COOKING WITH FISH

Marshall Cavendish

Picture Credits

Alan Duns: 7, 8, 10, 32/3, 34, 36/7, 38/9, 71, 72/3, 74/5, 76/7, 78, 118/9

Melvin Grey: 50/1, 69, 79, 82/3, 85

Anthony Kay: 87, 88/9, 90/1, 93, 95, 96/7, 99, 102, 104/5, 109

Paul Kemp: 2/3, 11, 12/3, 14/5, 16, 17, 18, 20, 21, 22/3, 24/5, 31, 106/7, 110

David Levin: 1, 4/5, 26/7, 29, 46/7, 61, 62/3, 80/1, 90/1, 112, 113, 115, 116, 120, 121, 126/7

Roger Phillips: 68

Paul Radkai: 64/5, 67

Paul Williams: 52, 54/5, 56/7, 58/9, 60, 100/1, 122/3

George Wright: 41, 42/3, 44/5, 48/9, 124/5, 128

Time symbols: an indication of preparation and cooking time is given for each recipe. This is calculated for beginners new to the techniques involved: experienced cooks need allow less time.

 less than 1 hour

 1-2½ hours

 Over 2½ hours

Published by
Marshall Cavendish Books Limited
58 Old Compton Street
London W1V 5PA

© Marshall Cavendish Limited 1976 - 1986

ISBN 0 85685 153 1

Printed and bound in Hong Kong
by Dai Nippon Printing Company

CONTENTS

On the line

Flat fish, round fish, oily fish, white fish—a confusion of fish and full of bones. So why do we bother to eat fish? Well, think of a tasty, golden grilled fish fillet served with a wedge of lemon—tempting and good for you as it's absolutely full of protein with low-fat content. Whatever your preference there is a fish for you whether it is whole, boned and stuffed, cut into steaks and cutlets or filleted. Here we take away all the nonsense which is talked about round white fish.

Absolutely fresh, inshore white fish has such a marvellous delicacy of flavour that it is a pity to smother it with added flavours. If you are lucky enough to have such fish, simply grill and baste it with butter and lemon juice or a maître d'hôtel butter. Less tasty fish from distant waters, perhaps frozen after landing, respond excellently to additional flavours including such strong ones as cheese, onion, garlic, tomato and anchovy.

Although fish and frying are almost synonymous, in fact grilling is often a better way of cooking fish. Not only is it a quick, clean and convenient method but it also seals in the flavour and prevents the loss of salts and nutrients.

Small, oily fish are excellent grilled whole or split, and grilling is the tastiest way of cooking white fish fillets and steaks.

Apart from dividing fish into white and oily categories, fish are also flat or round shaped. All oily fish are round but white fish can be flat, such as sole, or round, such as cod. Strictly speaking, the term round fish applies to all cylindrical fish as opposed to flat fish, such as sole, plaice and skate.

A selection of white fish and oily fish includes mackerel, sprats, red monk fish, sole, John Dory and haddock.

1 Cod
2 Gurnard
3 Rock salmon
4 Haddock
5 Whiting
6 Monk fish
7 Hake

ROUND WHITE FISH

The term white fish is most commonly associated with the familiar cod, coley, haddock, hake and whiting. But, in effect, it is simply a generic term covering all fish containing less than 2 per cent. oil. This small amount of oil is usually concentrated in the liver of the fish and the flesh is very lean. White fish is excellent for people on a low-fat diet. It is easy to digest, hence its association with convalescent diets.

Round white fish include bass, bream and gurnard, the less familiar pollock, pout and ling, as well as the more familiar ones which are usually available all year round and include the following:

Cod is a large white-fleshed fish which can weigh as much as 34 kg [75 lb]. Small cod are sold whole, but most shoppers buy cod already cut up into fillets, steaks or cutlets. These are sometimes frozen and fillets are available smoked. Cod grills well but, because its natural flavour is rather bland, it is best to serve the grill with a well-flavoured sauce or cooked with herbs so that it becomes more interesting and raises its status.

Coley, also known as saithe, is a member of the cod family and as the price of cod rises it is being used more and more as an alternative. It has off-white flesh when raw, which deters some people, but it turns white when cooked. It is sold skinned and filleted and, like cod but even more than cod, it needs a sauce or the addition of herbs to make it more interesting.

Gurnard, also called gurnet, is a small, tasty fish with firm white flesh. It is sold whole or filleted, is more tasty than cod and therefore needs less help to improve its flavour. It can be grilled and baked and is also particularly good eaten cold with salads.

Haddock belongs to the cod family, it is popular smoked but is also sold fresh whole, filleted or as steaks. It can be used for grilling and baking as well as in made-up dishes.

Hake is a tender fish with few bones and is sold as fillets and cutlets. It is a very tasty fish with flaky flesh and lends itself to any method of cooking with the minimum of fuss.

Whiting is a member of the cod family and is available all year round. It can be purchased whole or in fillets and is suited to baking and grilling. It is particularly good with a savoury stuffing, in which case it can be boned although this is not essential.

CHOOSING FISH

Don't be put off buying fish because you are not sure how to prepare it. Fishmongers are pleased to advise you about buying and preparing and they will usually prepare the fish for you without further charge, that is they will scale, behead, skin and fillet fish or divide it into steaks and cutlets as you require. However, these jobs are not difficult and step-by-step instructions are given to make them even simpler.

The sooner fish is cooked after catching the better it will taste. So always look first for signs of freshness. Fresh fish is at its very best when in season and plentiful, and the price should be cheaper then too. Medium-sized fish are likely to have a finer flavour and texture than larger specimens which tend to become coarse. Choose plump thick fish or fillets in preference to thin ones.

The following guidelines will help you to spot the freshest fish on the fishmonger's slab. In general, a firm shining appearance and clean fresh smell is essential. Any sign of dullness or flabbiness is a sign of age.

Whole fish: gills should be bright red—they darken and brown with age. The eyes must be bright and clear—they become dull and sunken with age. The skin must be moist and glistening, with clear colours. Dryness is a sign of age.

Fillets, cutlets and steaks: the flesh should look firm and bright—spongy texture denotes poor quality.

Frozen fish: buy where you know the turnover is brisk. See that packs are fresh looking and unbroken. Transparent bags of separate fillets are very useful because you can take out the number of fillets needed for one meal and grill them from their frozen state without having to thaw them first. Cook frozen fillets under low heat and for a longer time than when cooking fresh fillets.

QUANTITIES

Fish vary greatly in size, but all round fish have a general similarity in shape. Not all cuts are suitable for every type of fish—cutlets, for example, require a larger fish. However, the fishmonger applies the same methods of cutting to all fish, whether large or small. For example, if fillets are required the filleting is done in the same way whether it involves a large cod or a small whiting.

Small fish are usually sold whole. If a fish weighs less than 450 g [1 lb] it can be grilled whole for one person. This may sound a lot but·remember that the head, tail and bones account for quite a bit of the weight. Fish weighing 450-1 kg [1-2½ lb] are usually used for stuffing and baking, or they are filleted.

Medium-sized fish weighing about 1-2.3 kg [2½-5 lb] can be cooked whole and then be divided at table to serve several people but, for the purposes of grilling, a fish of this size is usually filleted before cooking to provide one long fillet from each side of the backbone. Each fillet, depending on size, can be divided into a number of portions. It is not necessary to buy whole fillets; the fishmonger will cut off as much as you require.

Large fish are usually cut crosswise to provide cutlets and steaks. The tail piece is sold for roasting or baking, or it may be filleted. The tail can also be poached, depending on the type of fish.

How much to buy

People's appetites vary enormously but, as a rough guide, any one of the following will provide enough for a main dish for one adult:

Fish fillets—150-175 g [5-6 oz] because every bit can be eaten.

Fish steaks or cutlets—175-200 g [6-7 oz]—slightly more than for fillets to allow for the bones.

One small whole fish—250-350 g [9-12 oz]. Additional weight here allows for head, tail and bones.

Large whole fish—allow 225 g [½ lb] per portion. This allows for the head and tail wastage and the weight of steaks or cutlets cut from a large whole fish should be as above.

PREPARATION FOR COOKING

When you get home after having bought the fish, unwrap it and rinse under cold running water, and drain thoroughly.

Lightly sprinkle the fish with cooking salt and lay it on a wire rack or on an inverted plate standing in a tray (this prevents the fish from standing in any liquid that drains from it). Cover loosely with polythene or foil and leave in a cold place, preferably the refrigerator under the frozen food compartment away from any other food that could possibly absorb the odour.

Keeping fish is not recommended; generally it should be cooked on the day of purchase and should never be kept for longer than 24 hours.

If the fishmonger has prepared the fish for you no further work is necessary; if not you will have to scale, gut, behead and fillet or bone the fish as required, depending on recipe.

Ideally, the fish should be prepared as close to cooking time as possible. However, this is not always convenient and if done a few hours in advance no harm will be done, but do cover the fish loosely with polythene and keep it chilled until it is required for cooking.

Scaling, gutting and boning or filleting a fish are messy jobs, but really very quick and easy to do once you know how.

If you want to stuff a fish and grill it whole, it is best to bone it (remove the backbone) so that the stuffing can be inserted into the cavity created. Removing the backbone is optional—the fish can be stuffed without boning—but it does give extra room so that you can use more stuffing, and it also makes eating easier. Boning is different from filleting in that the latter separates the fish into two halves, whereas boning removes the backbone without dividing the fish into two pieces. To bone a fish the initial preparation is the same as for filleting (see steps 1-5) although removing head and tail is optional, then proceed from step 11.

●The basic tools you will need are a sharp knife and a wooden or glass chopping board. The board must be clean and dry to prevent the fish from slipping.

●It is a good idea to rub both the working surface and your hands with a cut lemon afterwards to get rid of any fishy smells.

●Use the blunt side of the knife or a granton-edged knife for scaling.

●Have a roll of kitchen paper towels at the ready to blot up excess water after gutting and rinsing.

●Skinning fish is made easier if you first dip your thumb and forefinger in salt because this helps to give you a firm grip on the skin.

1 To scale, hold fish by tail and use blunt side of knife to scrape scales off towards the head.

5 To remove the tail, cut through the fish at its thinnest part. Cut off the head just behind the gills.

9 To skin a fresh fillet work a knife between the skin and flesh at tail end. Work skin away by hand.

Step-by-step filleting, boning and skinning fish

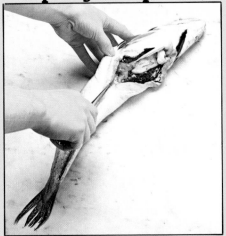

2 To gut fish, make a slit along the belly from below the gills along two-thirds of the body length.

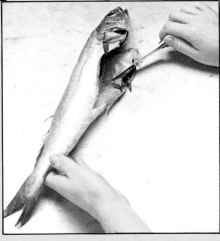

3 Scrape out inside of belly. Rub cavity with salt and scrape away black skin inside cavity.

4 Cut off the gill covers (the little fins behind the head) on both sides of the fish.

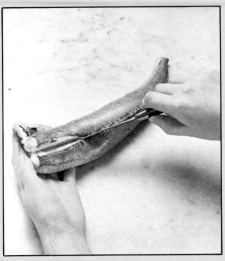

6 To fillet, cut along the backbone down to the tail end. Cut into the flesh, not just through the skin.

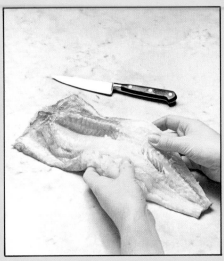

7 Cut the fish from belly cavity to tail and open it out flat by easing the belly cavity open.

8 Lift out the backbone from the head end. Ease the flesh from the backbone. Cut fillets in half.

10 To skin a frozen fillet lay the fish flesh side down and pull off skin from tail end.

11 To bone, press the fish, belly side down, along its backbone to open slightly without halving it.

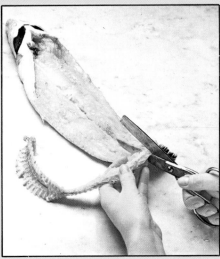

12 Cut through the bone at head end and ease away the backbone. Cut through at tail end and lift clear.

GRILLING WHITE FISH

Grilling is a particularly good method of cooking members of the round fish family. Because white fish do not contain much oil, for normal diets they should be grilled with added fat to prevent them from drying out during cooking.

There are various ways of adding extra fat when grilling fish.

1 Dot with butter and baste frequently during grilling time.
2 Marinate in flavoured oil before cooking and use the marinade as a baste when grilling.
3 Spread with a savoury topping containing fat and baste during grilling.
4 Use a savoury butter and baste during grilling time.

Salt is a great ally of white fish. This is not surprising as these fish come from the sea. The flavour of fish benefits enormously if the cut surfaces are liberally sprinkled with salt before cooking. Pepper can be added too if you like.

Temperature

Skinned fresh fish should be grilled under medium heat and skinned frozen fish under medium-low heat. Wet skin is unpleasant to eat and is a major reason why some people

dislike fish. Medium heat is not sufficient to cook the skin thoroughly. So, when grilling fish with its skin on, the secret recipe for really crisp and tasty results is to grill under fierce heat initially.

Fillets need not be skinned for grilling. In fact the skin makes the fillets easier to handle and less likely to break up. Grill fillets skin side up for a couple of minutes. Do this under fierce heat and do it first. Then reduce heat to medium, turn the fish carefully and cook the cut side. A fish slice and palette knife are the best implements for turning fish without breaking it.

Grilling times

Fish cooks extremely quickly, much quicker than many people imagine, and it is all too easy to overcook it. So do stay close to the grill when cooking fish and time things so that diners are ready to eat as soon as the fish is cooked.

It is always a pity to overcook fish because it dries out, becomes unappetizingly chewy and loses its delicate flavour— so good food goes to waste and all your labour has been in vain.

When grilling whole fish, steaks and cutlets, watch for the moment when the skin starts shrinking and then check that the flesh is opaque and comes cleanly away from the bone. This is a sure sign that the fish is cooked, so remove it from the grill immediately.

Fillets are cooked when the flesh is opaque right through to the skin. And if the fish is really fresh you will see a white creamy substance oozing out between the flakes.

Exact times vary depending on the size of the fish, but here is a guide for fresh fish. (Allow slightly longer for frozen fish.)

Grill fillets for a total 8-10 minutes, cutlets and steaks for 6-12 minutes each side depending on thickness, and 6-10 minutes each side for whole or stuffed round fish.

Turn cutlets, steaks and whole fish during grilling so that both sides will cook through. Also turn fillets which are cooked with the skin on. Skinned fillets do not need turning.

MONTE CARLO COD STEAKS

This is a colourful way of bringing a little Mediterranean flavour to any type of white fish steaks or cutlets, fresh or frozen. Garnish with chopped parsley.

SERVES 4
4 cod steaks
30 ml [2 tablespoons] oil
450 g [1 lb] ripe tomatoes
15 ml [1 tablespoon]
  finely chopped onion
1 small garlic clove, crushed
salt
black pepper
5 ml [1 teaspoon] sugar
2.5 ml [½ teaspoon] oregano
  or thyme
4 anchovy fillets

1 Put the tomatoes into boiling water for 1 minute, drain and refresh in cold water. Skin, cut in half and squeeze out the seeds. Chop the flesh into rough pieces.

2 Heat half the oil in a small saucepan, add the onion, cover and sweat over a low heat for about 5 minutes.

3 Stir in the garlic and cook for another minute.

4 Stir in the tomatoes, raise the heat and cook until the tomatoes are soft and most of their liquid has evaporated, about 5-10 minutes. Season to taste with salt, pepper and sugar.

5 Heat the grill to medium heat.

6 Choose a shallow flame-proof dish into which the fish will fit in a single layer. Heat the remaining oil in it.

7 Season the fish fairly liberally with salt and pepper on each side, place in the dish and turn so that each side is lightly coated with oil.

8 Grill the fish on each side for 4 minutes. Meanwhile, cut each anchovy fillet in half lengthways.

9 Spread each portion of fish with the tomato mixture and sprinkle a little oregano or thyme on top. Add the anchovy fillets, arranging them criss-cross fashion over the top of each fish steak.

10 Continue grilling for another 3-4 minutes until the fish is cooked through.

Handy hints

● Lemon juice, of course, is a perfect foil for all kinds of fish. It counteracts the richness of oily fish and heightens the flavour of white fish. Make it a golden rule when buying fish to buy a lemon at the same time.

● Glass working surfaces are excellent for fish as they do not retain the smell afterwards. The best type has a raised dimple surface to prevent the fish from slipping while you are working and to raise it up from the blood which escapes when the fish is gutted.

● When using a wooden chopping board cover it with several layers of paper (newspaper will do). This makes cleaning up afterwards easier and also prevents the chopping board from absorbing the fish flavour which could spoil other foods.

FISH FILLETS IN MORNAY SAUCE

Any fish fillets can be used for this dish and you can vary it by using fish steaks or cutlets instead of the fillets. Initial grilling time is slightly shorter than usual because the fish will continue cooking when it is covered with sauce and browned under grill.

SERVES 4
700 g [1½ lb] white fish fillets
15 ml [1 tablespoon] butter
salt and black pepper

For the Mornay sauce:
half a small onion
half a small carrot
quarter of a celery stalk
250 ml [½ pt] milk
bay leaf
62 g [2½ oz] butter
25 g [1 oz] flour
salt and white pepper
pinch of nutmeg
50 g [2 oz] Gruyère or
Parmesan cheese

For the topping:
25 g [1 oz] Cheddar or
Gruyère cheese

1 Prepare the vegetables, put into a pan and add the milk and bay leaf. Season and bring to the boil. Remove from the heat, cover and leave to infuse for 30 minutes. Then strain the milk and reheat gently.

2 Grate the cheese. Heat the grill to fierce heat and butter a flame-proof dish.

3 Melt 25 g [1 oz] of the butter in a pan over low heat. Remove from the heat and stir in the flour. Return to the heat and stir to a smooth paste.

4 Remove the pan from the heat and add the milk, stirring continuously. Bring to the boil, stirring, and then cover and simmer for 5 minutes.

Sprigs of parsley add a touch of green to fish fillets smothered under a lightly browned Mornay sauce.

5 Season the fish fillets. Place them in a single layer in the gratin dish, skin side up. Grill for 2 minutes to crisp the skin.

6 Carefully turn the fillets over with a fish slice, reduce heat to medium and continue grilling for 2 minutes.

7 Meanwhile, remove the sauce from the heat and stir into it 50 g [2 oz] cheese and the remaining butter.

8 Remove the gratin dish from under the grill and increase heat again to fierce.

9 Pour the Mornay sauce over the fish fillets. Sprinkle the remaining grated cheese on top.

10 Brown quickly under the grill and serve immediately.

CARNIVAL FISH KEBABS

Use thick fillets of firm white fish, such as gurnard, monk fish or rock salmon as well as coley and cod. Thick fillets are used so that they can be cut into the 2.5 cm (1") cubes required. A bed of boiled rice coloured with turmeric, or sweet corn topped with crumbled crispy bacon, goes well with this colourful dish. Serve the kebabs garnished with wedges of lemon.

SERVES 3
450 g [1 lb] fish fillets
1 large green pepper
100 g [¼ lb] cap mushrooms
1 garlic clove
6 bay leaves
6 small firm tomatoes

For the marinade:
45 ml [3 tablespoons] olive oil
30 ml [2 tablespoons] lemon juice
salt and black pepper
5 ml [1 teaspoon] dried oregano

1 Remove the skin from the fillets by easing it away from the flesh with a knife, then pulling gently with your fingers.

2 Cut the flesh into 2.5 cm [1"] cubes.

3 Cut the pepper in half, remove the stalk and seeds and blanch. To do this, put the pepper into a basin, cover with boiling water, leave for 5 minutes and then drain.

4 Cut the pepper into 2.5 cm [1"] squares.

5 Wipe the mushrooms clean with damp kitchen paper and trim stalks level with caps.

6 Mix all the marinade ingredients together in a basin and add the fish, green pepper and mushroom caps. Stir to coat the ingredients thoroughly. Cover and refrigerate for 2 hours. Stir once or twice during this time.

7 Rub kebab skewers with oil, then rub each skewer with a halved garlic clove to pick up the flavour.

Fish kebabs served on a bed of yellow rice and garnished with wedges of lemon makes a colourful and appetizing meal.

8 Drain the kebab ingredients from the marinade, reserving marinade. Thread pieces of fish, pepper and mushroom caps on to the skewers. Continue until all the ingredients have been used, including two bay leaves on each skewer.

9 Heat the grill pan with the grid in position to medium heat.

10 Put the kebabs on the grid and cook for 12 minutes, turning the skewers and basting with the marinade several times.

11 Slip the tomatoes on the ends of the skewers for the last 5 minutes of cooking time.

12 Heat any remaining marinade in a small pan.

13 Transfer the fish to a warmed serving dish and pour the heated marinade and pan juices over the fish. Garnish and serve immediately.

GOLDEN GRILL FISH FILLETS

A blanket of tangy creamed cheese keeps the fish beneath it beautifully moist and succulent, and is an excellent way to add zest to fish with a bland flavour. It is a good way of cooking any type of white fish fillets, steaks or cutlets—frozen or fresh—but remember to adjust temperature and timing accordingly if deviating from the basic recipe. Use equal quantities of Gruyère and Parmesan for a subtle flavour or Cheddar cheese to give a more robust flavour.

SERVES 4
4 cod fillets each weighing 150-175 g [5-6 oz]
salt and pepper
25 g [1 oz] butter
4 tomatoes
parsley sprigs

For the topping:
150 g [5 oz] grated cheese
15 ml [1 tablespoon] French mustard
30 ml [2 tablespoons] thin cream or top of milk

1 Choose a large, shallow flame-proof dish in which the fillets can lie side by side in a single layer, and in which they can be served.

2 Heat the grill to a fierce heat and melt the butter in the flame-proof dish.

3 Season the fish fillets by sprinkling them generously with salt and pepper.

4 Lay the fillets cut side down in the melted butter in the dish and grill under high heat for 2 minutes to crisp the skin.

5 Meanwhile put the cheese and mustard into a basin and beat in the cream to make a soft easily spread mixture.

6 Turn the fillets carefully with a fish slice and spread the cheese mixture evenly all over the cut side.

7 Reduce heat and grill under a medium heat (or lower the grill pan) for 6-8 minutes depending on the thickness of the fillets.

8 Cut the tomatoes in half and arrange, cut side up, around the fish for the last 5 minutes of grilling.

9 Do not let the dish overbrown. When cooked the surface should be a mottled golden brown all over. Garnish with parsley and serve immediately.

Variations

Substitute one of the following in place of the creamed cheese topping:
● For a caper grill, mix 45 ml [3 tablespoons] olive oil, 22 ml [1½ tablespoons] wine vinegar, 15 ml [1 tablespoon] drained and chopped capers, 15 ml [1 tablespoon] chopped pickled gherkins and salt and pepper to taste. Pour over the cut side of the fish and baste frequently while cooking. Sprinkle with chopped parsley just before serving.
● For a garden grill melt 50 g [2 oz] butter, add 30 ml [2 tablespoons] lemon juice and 45 ml [3 tablespoons] grated onion. Pour over the cut side of the fish and baste while cooking. Sprinkle with finely chopped chives before serving.
● For a devilled grill, melt 50 g [2 oz] butter, add 10 ml [2 teaspoons] curry powder, 15 ml [1 tablespoon] fruit chutney and 15 ml [1 tablespoon] French mustard. Mix the ingredients and spread over the cut side of the fish. Baste during grilling.

2 whiting, each weighing
  350-450 g [¾-1 lb]
salt and black pepper
15 ml [1 tablespoon] butter

For the stuffing:
75 g [3 oz] butter, at
  room temperature
40 g [1½ oz] white breadcrumbs
30 ml [2 tablespoons] freshly
  chopped mixed herbs such
  as parsley, chives, balm
  and mint
salt
black pepper
1 lemon

1 Butter a flame-proof gratin dish.

2 Skin the fillets by easing a knife under the skin and gently pulling the skin away.

3 Cut each fillet in half lengthways so that you have a total of 8 fillets.

4 Heat the grill to medium heat and prepare the stuffing. First beat the butter in a small bowl until smooth and creamy.

5 Add the herbs and breadcrumbs.

6 Grate the lemon zest and add to the stuffing. Season with salt and pepper and mix well.

7 Squeeze the juice from the lemon and add a few drops to the stuffing, if required, to give it a spreading consistency.

8 Divide stuffing into 8 portions.

9 Using a round-bladed knife, spread each fillet lengthways with a portion of stuffing.

10 Roll up from the tail end and secure with a skewer or cocktail stick.

11 Place the rolled fish fillets in the buttered gratin dish, laying them flat in a single layer. Pour over the remaining lemon juice.

12 Grill under medium heat for 5 minutes and then turn each fillet over using a fish slice.

13 Grill for a further 5-8 minutes until the fish is cooked. Serve immediately.

PINWHEEL WHITING GRILL

Ask the fishmonger to clean and fillet the fish for you, or prepare them yourself following the step-by-step instructions given. The two fillets from each fish are divided lengthways into two and spread with stuffing before being rolled and grilled. Secure the pinwheels with poultry skewers or with wooden cocktail sticks. If using cocktail sticks, trim any protruding

Fillets of whiting are stuffed with a mixture of herbs, butter and breadcrumbs for a pinwheel grill.

ends or they may char when placed under the grill.

Fresh herbs are best for the stuffing. Use any that are available. The butter in the stuffing keeps the fish moist during grilling.

A fishy story

Oily fish include both sea and freshwater fish; they have darker flesh and are richer than white fish. They grill very well and have a great affinity with piquant sauces made from tart fruit such as gooseberries. Here we include details of oily fish and how to grill and serve them with sauces and savoury butters.

OILY FISH

The definition 'oily' is given to fish which have an oil content of between five per cent and 15 per cent. The oil is distributed throughout the flesh instead of being concentrated in the liver, as is the case of white fish (see pages 1–3). Oily fish include herring, mackerel, eel, salmon, sprats, sardines and mullet, among others. The flesh of all these fish is darker in colour than white fish and, as you might expect, they are richer to eat. In fact, some people have difficulty in digesting oily fish, so grilling is a better way of cooking.

Whereas white fish can be either flat or round, all oily fish are round. Some oily fish are seasonal but the more common and popular ones are available all year round, either fresh or frozen. Frozen oily fish should not be kept for more than 2 months.

Carp is a freshwater fish with a muddy flavour. To counteract this soak it in salted water for at least three hours before cooking it. There are different varieties and sizes—small fish can be grilled whole but a larger fish is better baked or poached, with or without stuffing.

Common eel is a freshwater fish. It can be smoked or jellied, and it is also available fresh. It is displayed at the fishmongers alive. The fishmonger will kill it for you on purchase or you can take it home alive—it should be cooked as soon as possible after killing. It is tasty and can be fried, grilled or poached and is also particularly suitable for fish soups and stews.

Grey mullet is not related to red mullet. It is fatty and can be grilled although large grey mullet is better baked, poached or fried rather than grilled.

Herring is a salt-water fish and is eaten by most people in the form of kippers. It is also available salted and as rollmops and buckling. Herring is sold fresh, usually whole, and is very tasty. This is a very versatile fish but it is at its best simply grilled and served with a savoury butter. Soft herring roes are sold separately and these too can be grilled or poached.

Mackerel is a salt-water fish. It may be smoked and, of all oily fish, it is probably the most popular for grilling (being cheaper than trout). Mackerel goes off very quickly and should therefore be bought as fresh as possible and cooked on the day of purchase. It can be served hot or cold.

Pilchards are small salt-water fish and are seldom available fresh as they do not keep at all well and are therefore canned.

Red mullet is a salt-water fish with a delicate flavour and distinctive for its close texture. Small fish are delicious grilled whole. Mullet can also be baked, poached or fried.

Salmon is a salt-water fish which spawns in fresh water. It is probably best known to most people in its canned form and also its smoked. Fresh salmon is available as steaks and cutlets. Tail-end pieces can be baked or poached whole. Salmon is of all fish the most highly prized. It is tasty and has a distinctive texture and appearance. It is also expensive, but a great treat for an occasional splurge.

Sea or salmon trout is smaller than salmon. Although no relation to the salmon, it is similar in appearance—hence its name. It is more delicate in flavour, and it is usually baked or poached, but may be substituted for salmon in salmon recipes.

Sprats are small salt-water fish related to the herring family. They are often fried but can be grilled for a light snack and are a cheap alternative to whitebait.

Trout is a freshwater fish which has become so popular that it is specially reared on fish farms. It can be smoked. Fresh trout is usually gutted and grilled or fried whole for one serving.

Whitebait is the fry (or young) of herring and sprats and is made up of a mass of these tiny silver fish. Whitebait is best deep-fried whole, complete with heads and backbones, and served as an appetizer.

CHOOSING FISH

Oily fish are sold in the same cuts as white fish: whole, as steaks or as cutlets or fillets, depending on the size of the fish. Always look for signs of freshness. Gills, eyes and skin should be bright. Any sign of dullness denotes poor quality and should be avoided. Scaly fish, such as herring, should have plenty of scales. Fillets, cutlets and steaks should look firm and bright. In addition to the above, oily fish should be 'stiff alive', as the fishermen say, and not floppy when picked up.

Quantities and preparation of oily fish are the same as for round white fish (see on pages 3–5). Remember that it is always important to look for signs of freshness and to cook fish on the day of purchase. When grilling fish whole, it is optional whether you remove the head and tail but the fish looks better served with them; the diners then remove the flesh from the bones on the dinner plate. If, however, the fish is to be split open and laid out flat, the head should be removed. Most oily fish are cleaned, boned and filleted in the same way as round white fish.

You are more likely to find roes in herring and mackerel than in white fish. Leave the roe in the fish or combine it with a stuffing. If you have sufficient quantity, roes can be grilled separately.

Herring has a lot of scales and mackerel has none, but as mackerel has a larger belly than herring the overall cleaning time will remain the same.

GRILLING OILY FISH

Whole oily fish to be grilled must be given a few oblique slits along each side. These slits prevent the fish from splitting because the flesh contracts as it cooks, pulling away from the skin. It also allows the heat to penetrate for even cooking. Make three or four cuts 2.5 cm [1"] apart in the body on each side.

Apart from an initial brushing with oil to help crisp the skin and prevent the fish from sticking to the grid, no additional fat is needed. Oily fish are at their best well seasoned with salt and pepper plus, if you wish, a little lemon juice or wine vinegar. Serve with a tangy sauce to counteract the richness.

Grilling time depends on the size and therefore the thickness of the fish—do not overcook fish as they will dry out. Fresh fish cook slightly quicker than frozen fish. Generally fish are grilled under a medium heat but, to crisp the skin on fillets, grilling is started under a fierce heat which is then reduced after about two minutes or the pan is lowered.

Split fish, steaks and cutlets cook more quickly than whole round fish and can be grilled closer to the heat or under a slightly higher heat. Grill fillets for 3-5 minutes each side. The skin is left on as it does help to hold the fillet together. Grill the skin side first under a fierce heat for 2 minutes to dry it out. Reduce heat and continue grilling. Turn the fillet over with a fish slice and finish the cooking. Cutlets and steaks need to be cooked for 6-10 minutes on each side, depending on thickness.

Small whole round fish weighing up to 450 g [1 lb] need 6-12 minutes under a medium heat on each side.

Larger fish should be grilled at a slightly lower temperature long enough for the heat to penetrate the thickest part of the fish.

Ridged-pan grilling

Fish can be pan grilled or 'dry fried'. A very thick frying pan made of iron or cast aluminium is essential or, better still, is a ridged iron pan which gives fish a 'quadrilled' surface.

Heat the pan over a high heat for a few minutes until it is thoroughly hot. Grease the pan with a piece of hard fat impaled on a fork, or brush the pan with oil. Use just enough oil to give a thin film of grease. Pour off any surplus. When the oil is sizzling put the seasoned fish in the pan. Grill the fish but decrease the cooking time by about 1 minute on each side.

A variety of oily fish—1 Carp. 2 Herring. 3 Sprats. 4 Red mullet. 5 Eel. 6 Whitebait. 7 Trout. 8 Grey mullet. 9 Mackerel.

SAVOURY BUTTERS

These are an excellent way of adding both fat and flavouring to fish. Oily fish do not need the extra fat so much as white fish but the herbs or other flavouring in the butter make the fish more interesting, while the butter provides a little sauce at the same time.

Use chilled pats of butter to top the cooked fish, or use the savoury butter as a stuffing, or put it on the fish half-way through cooking time and, as it melts, use it to baste the fish. Be sure to pour the buttery juices from the pan over the fish just before serving.

The savoury butters mentioned in previous courses may be used but the following are particularly good with oily fish:
● For mustard butter, cream 50 g [2 oz] unsalted butter with 10 ml [2 teaspoons] French mustard. Season with salt and pepper.
● For mustard and watercress butter, add 15 ml [1 tablespoon] finely chopped watercress to a mustard butter. Use this for a topping only and not as a baste.
● For anise butter, cream 50 g [2 oz] unsalted butter with 10-15 ml [2-3 teaspoons] Pernod, pastis or Ricard. This is an interesting flavour with fish.

SAUCES

The best sauces for rich oily fish such as mackerel and herring are ones that contrast sharply in flavour and texture and reduce the richness of the fish.

GOOSEBERRY SAUCE

This is best made from early season cooking gooseberries which are still very sharp and fresh tasting. It is a perfect foil for grilled mackerel.

SERVES 4
225 g [½ lb] green gooseberries
15 ml [1 tablespoon] white sugar
10 ml [2 teaspoons] butter
pinch of grated nutmeg

1 Top and tail the gooseberries and rinse in cold water.

2 Put into a small heavy-based saucepan with 60 ml [4 table-spoons] water and leave un-covered. Stew gently for 10-15

minutes until all the gooseberries become soft. Then allow to cool a little.

3 Reduce to a puree in a liquidizer. For a rough-textured sauce, break up the gooseberries to release the juice by beating briskly with a small wire whisk.

4 Return to the saucepan, reheat and add the sugar, butter and nutmeg. Serve hot or cold.

Variations

Substitute one of the following for the gooseberries.
● For rhubarb sauce: use young rhubarb and, instead of nutmeg, a piece of finely grated orange zest.
● For damson sauce: use damsons and remove stones from the cooked fruit with a spoon before reducing to a purée.

Grilled whole herring is accompanied by parsnips—a tasty Scottish custom. Apple and horseradish cream is an uncooked sauce.

APPLE AND HORSERADISH CREAM

This is a delicately sharp, uncooked sauce especially suited to grilled herring and is also good with mackerel.

SERVES 4
1 large cooking apple
15 ml [1 tablespoon] lemon juice
15 ml [1 tablespoon] horseradish sauce
45 ml [3 tablespoons] thick cream or sour cream

1 Quarter the apple, cut out the core and grate the flesh including the skin on the coarse side of a grater.

2 Immediately add the lemon juice and stir to mix thoroughly.

3 Stir in the horseradish and the cream and serve.

GRILLED WHOLE HERRING

There is no better way of cooking herring than grilling. Vinegar is spooned into cuts in the fish to counteract the rich oiliness of the herring.

Eating parsnips with herring is a Scottish custom—the flavours do go together very well. Instead of boiling the parsnips as given in the recipe, they can be steamed; for this method chop them into pieces as steaming whole parsnips takes a long time.

Serve the grilled herring with apple and horseradish cream or a mustard sauce.

SERVES 4
**4 fresh herring weighing
    225-350 g [$\frac{1}{2}$-$\frac{3}{4}$ lb] each
700 g [$1\frac{1}{2}$ lb] parsnips
15 ml [1 tablespoon] cooking oil
salt and black pepper
15 ml [1 tablespoon] wine
    vinegar
2.5 ml [$\frac{1}{2}$ teaspoon] caraway
    seeds (optional)
30 ml [2 tablespoons] butter**

1 Scrub the parsnips under cold running water.

2 If the fishmonger has not already done so, prepare the herring by scaling and gutting it. Wash outside and inside under running water, and blot dry.

3 Fill a large pan one-third full of water. Add salt and bring to the boil.

4 Add the parsnips to the boiling water. Cover and simmer for 20 minutes.

5 Cut 3 oblique slits on each side along the length of each fish.

6 Heat the grill pan to a medium heat with the grill pan and grid in position.

7 Brush the fish with oil and season with salt and pepper.

8 Lay the fish on the grid and spoon a few drops of vinegar into each of the exposed cuts.

9 Grill for about 6 minutes.

10 Turn the fish gently, spoon a few drops of vinegar into the cuts and continue grilling for 6-8 minutes until the fish is cooked.

11 Drain the parsnips as soon as they are cooked. Chop them into bite-sized pieces.

12 Melt the butter in the empty pan. Add the parsnip pieces and shake the pan so that they are covered on all sides with the butter. Grind over a generous quantity of black pepper.

13 Arrange the parsnips round the edge of a large serving dish and sprinkle over the caraway seeds. Put the herrings in the middle.

BROILED SPLIT MACKEREL

Serve gooseberry sauce with this dish as the sauce is the perfect complement to the richness of plainly grilled mackerel. If gooseberries are out of season, use another fruit such as damsons or, even, rhubarb.

SERVES 4
**4 fresh mackerel weighing
    225-350 g [$\frac{1}{2}$-$\frac{3}{4}$ lb] each
salt and pepper
15 ml [1 tablespoon] cooking oil**

**For the garnish:
gooseberry sauce
sprigs of parsley or watercress**

1 If the fishmonger has not already prepared the fish, cut off the gill covers on both sides of each fish and remove the heads.

2 Make a slit along the belly cavity to two-thirds of the length and gut the fish. Remove any black skin inside the cavity.

3 Wash the body cavity of the fish under running water and blot dry.

4 Cut the fish open from the belly cavity to the tail end. Press it along its backbone to open it without actually halving the fish.

5 Turn the fish over, and working from the head end, ease away the backbone from the flesh. Cut it free where it joins the tail, lift it out with as many bones as possible.

6 Sprinkle with salt and pepper and brush both sides with oil.

7 Heat the grill to a high heat with the grill pan and grid in position.

8 Lay the mackerel open on the grid so that the whole skin is exposed to the heat. Cook for 2 minutes to crisp the skin.

9 Reduce heat to medium and carefully turn the fish over. Grill for 4-6 minutes until cooked through.

10 Heat the gooseberry sauce in a small saucepan.

11 Serve the fish flesh side up on a heated plate with a little hot fruit sauce spooned down the centre of each fish. Garnish with parsley or watercress.

MACKEREL MARINATA

Fresh mackerel, marinated then grilled and served cold make a substantial but elegant main meal dish to serve with a crisp salad. The mackerel can be boned or left whole.

SERVES 4
4 fresh mackerel weighing about 225-350 g [$\frac{1}{2}$-$\frac{3}{4}$ lb] each

For the marinade:
45 ml [3 tablespoons] olive oil
45 ml [3 tablespoons] lemon juice
5 ml [1 teaspoon] salt
black pepper
1 bay leaf

For the garnish:
2 seedless oranges
50 g [2 oz] black olives
watercress sprigs

1 If the fishmonger has not already gutted the fish, make a slit along two-thirds of the body length. Scrape out the inside of belly cavity and remove black skin.

2 Wash the belly cavity under running water and blot dry.

3 Cut off the gill covers on both sides of each fish.

4 Cut the fish open from the belly cavity to the tail end. Press it along its backbone to open it without actually halving the fish.

5 Working from the head end, ease away the backbone from the fish. Cut it free at the head and tail ends. Lift it out with as many bones as possible and discard.

6 Cut a few oblique slits along the body length.

7 Place fish side by side in a flameproof dish.

8 Mix all the ingredients for the marinade together; pour it over the fish and spoon it into the body cavity. Cover and refrigerate for 2 hours turning the fish occasionally.

9 Heat the grill to a medium heat.

10 Uncover the fish, baste again with the marinade and place the dish under grill.

11 Cook for 6-8 minutes depending on size. Turn over carefully and grill for a further 6-8 minutes until the fish is cooked. Baste with pan juices during grilling time.

12 Set aside in a cool place until completely cold, basting occasionally.

13 To serve, arrange the fish on a flat platter and spoon a little of the marinade over them. Slice the oranges thinly and arrange around the fish with the olives and watercress sprigs.

GRILLED SPRATS

Sprats are inexpensive and make a tasty grill. The problem of turning so many small fish is solved by skewering them in a row like clothes on a line. Serve sprats on their own for a snack allowing 450 g [1 lb] for 3 portions—this will give about 7-8 fish per portion.

Serve with lemon wedges and brown bread and butter. Children will also enjoy grilled sprats. This dish can be served as a first course to a meal.

Sprats are small and the bones are soft enough to eat. There is no need to remove the head or tail as they are edible. Grill the sprats under a high heat to crisp the skins—the flesh cooks quickly because the fish are so small.

SERVES 3
450 g [1 lb] sprats
15 ml [1 tablespoon] oil
salt and black pepper

1 Wash the sprats under running cold water, then pat dry with kitchen paper.

2 Put them into a basin, add the oil, salt and pepper, and stir gently so that each fish is lightly coated with oil and seasoning.

3 Heat the grill to a high heat.

4 Thread the sprats through the heads on two or three metal skewers, spacing them out so that each fish will lie flat on the grid without overlapping—the grid allows surplus fat to drain away.

5 Grill close to a high heat until the skin is crisp and golden then carefully lift each skewer and turn it over to present the uncooked side of the sprats to the grill.

6 Grill for another 2-3 minutes until crisp and cooked through.

7 Ease the sprats off the skewer with a fork on to a hot serving dish. Garnish with lemons and serve.

Left: mackerel marinata is a colourful and substantial dish which is served cold.
Right: grilled sprats cooked on skewers make an enjoyable tea-time treat.

SALMON STEAKS FLORENTINE

This superb dish tastes as magnificent as it looks—and it's easy and quick to prepare too!

SERVES 4
4 salmon steaks about 2.5 cm [1"] thick
50 g [2 oz] unsalted butter
1 kg [2 lb] spinach
50 ml [2 fl oz] thick cream
salt and black pepper

For the sauce:
175 g [6 oz] unsalted butter
juice of half a lemon
salt and white pepper
cayenne pepper

1 Remove stems and discard any yellow leaves from the spinach.

2 Wash thoroughly and drain to remove excess water.

3 Heat the grill to a medium heat.

4 Season the salmon steaks.

5 Place the salmon on the grid of the grill pan and dot each steak with butter.

6 Grill for 8-10 minutes.

7 Meanwhile pack the spinach into a large pan and place it on a fairly high heat. Cover.

8 As soon as the spinach starts sizzling, turn it using a wooden spoon. Reduce the heat.

9 Turn the salmon steaks over and cook for 8-10 minutes, basting with the pan juices during this time.

10 Turn the spinach over in the pan; it will reduce in quantity as it cooks. Continue cooking for a total of 10-12 minutes.

11 Melt the butter for the sauce and add the lemon juice and seasonings.

12 Turn the cooked spinach into a colander and press with a spoon to extract any moisture.

Lemon twists add a decorative touch to salmon steaks which are served on a bed of spinach with a butter sauce.

13 Return to empty pan and add cream, salt and pepper. Mix together and transfer to a serving dish.

14 Transfer the cooked salmon steaks on to the spinach and pour the butter sauce over. Serve immediately.

KIPPERS GRILLED FACE TO FACE

Kipper cures vary a great deal from smoker to smoker so always ask the fishmonger the best method of cooking the particular brand he stocks. For mildly cured kippers grilling is best and the following way of cooking them in pairs keeps them especially moist and succulent. Allow 1 pair of kippers for 2 portions.

SERVES 2
1 pair of kippers
25 g [1 oz] butter at room temperature

1 Heat the grill to a medium heat.

2 Cut the heads off the kippers. Spread the flesh side of one kipper with half the softened butter. Lay the other kipper, flesh side down, on top of it, like a sandwich.

3 Lay on the grid and cook for about 5 minutes.

4 Using a fish slice turn the pair of kippers over and grill the other side for 5 minutes.

5 To serve, separate the kippers and arrange the butter side uppermost, with a pat of the remaining butter on each.

HERRING ROE TOASTS

To grill herring roes use the grill pan without the grid. If the grill pan is large, use a flame-proof dish instead as the pan or dish should be only large enough to hold the roes in a single layer.

SERVES 4
450 g [1 lb] soft herring roes
5 ml [1 teaspoon] curry powder
black pepper
2.5 ml [½ teaspoon] salt
15 ml [1 tablespoon] flour
65 g [2½ oz] butter
4 slices of bread

pinch paprika pepper
parsley sprigs

1 Heat the grill to a moderate heat with the grill pan in position but remove the grid.

2 Put the roes in a colander and rinse under cold water. Remove any black or silver threads.

3 Drain the roes on kitchen paper and blot dry.

4 Add the curry powder, pepper and salt to the flour and mix well. Roll roes in the seasoned flour until they are thoroughly covered.

5 Melt 40 g [1½ oz] butter in the grill pan or dish and, when hot, put in the roes. Turn them carefully with a spoon to coat them with butter.

6 Grill gently for about 5-6 minutes, turning and basting them now and then.

7 Cut the crusts from the bread. Place the slices on the grid and place the grid over the roes in the grill pan. Toast the bread on both sides.

8 Spread the toast with butter, arrange the roes on the toast and sprinkle lightly with paprika.

9 Garnish with parsley and serve very hot.

RED MULLET WITH FENNEL

Herring, mackerel and sea bream can also be used for this recipe. The essential thing is that the fish must be fresh. The dried fennel stalks impart a smoky aniseed fragrance to the fish.

SERVES 4
4 red mullet each weighing about 350 g [¾ lb]
3 dozen dried fennel stalks
40 g [1½ oz] butter at room temperature
15 ml [1 tablespoon] chopped parsley
15 ml [1 tablespoon] lemon juice
salt and black pepper
15 ml [1 tablespoon] oil
15 ml [1 tablespoon] brandy

1 Remove heads from the fish, gut, and bone them if you wish. Wash

and dry the fish. Score each side of each fish with 3 or 4 cuts along the body.

2 Heat the grill to a medium heat.

3 Stuff each fish with 6 fennel stalks. Place the remaining fennel stalks on a flame-proof serving dish and keep warm.

4 Mix together the butter, parsley and lemon juice and season generously with salt and pepper.

5 Fill the cuts in the fish with the butter mixture.

6 Brush the fish with oil and place on the grid of the grill pan.

7 Grill the fish for 6-10 minutes (depending on size) until the skin is crisp and golden.

8 Carefully turn the fish over and brush with oil and continue grilling for 6-10 minutes until the fish is cooked through.

9 Place the grid with the fish on it over the fennel stalks in the flame-proof serving dish.

10 Heat a metal tablespoon and pour the brandy into it. Set fire to the brandy and pour it over the fish. The fennel stalks will catch fire giving off smoke which imparts its flavour to the fish. Let the fish stand over the smoking stalks for 10 minutes before serving.

Variation
If fresh fennel is available, it makes an interesting variation instead of the dried stalks and the brandy.
● Cut the fennel stalks from the top of the bulb, and insert one into each fish. Cut the bulb into paper thin slices, sprinkle with oil, lemon juice and salt, and arrange it as a garnish round the fish.

Small red mullet—a salt-water fish—is close textured and has a delicate flavour.

Full steam ahead

For many people steamed fish conjures up images of invalid meals with portions of anaemic white fish languishing in a pool of pale, insipid sauce. Here we introduce flat fish and explain the secret of steaming fish to retain all its original flavour and nutrients as well as the preparation of skinning and filleting.

ADVANTAGES OF STEAMING

Steaming is one of the most popular ways of cooking fish in Chinese and Japanese cookery, where the art of adding colour and flavour, and presenting the fish attractively is thoroughly understood. It is a method which uses an absolute minimum of fuel, and where the same fuel can be used to cook other small pieces of food at the same time. This makes steaming a very convenient method for campers, caravanners or people living in limited accommodation, as well as for everyone trying to keep down fuel bills. Another advantage of this cooking method is that all the valuable nutrients in the fish are retained.

Bear in mind the following to serve fish at its best.

1 Use really fresh fish—steaming is a method which retains all the natural flavour, so the fresher the fish the better the results.

2 Season the fish well. Even the freshest fish is improved if sprinkled generously with salt, lightly with white pepper (the colour of white pepper looks more attractive than black with most fish) and finally, adding a good squeeze of lemon juice. This seasoning is best done immediately after preparation (cleaning and filleting) so that the flavours have a chance to penetrate during the time the fish

is kept in the refrigerator before it is cooked. Fine-flavoured fish, such as sole, halibut and John Dory need no other seasoning, but less tasty fish such as megrim or witch, benefit from more exotic seasonings, such as soy sauce and spices, which are added just before cooking.

3 Do not overcook fish. Fish cooks remarkably quickly so always time the cooking carefully (use a timer if necessary). Overcooking spoils the texture as well as the flavour. Steam fish in a single layer so that it cooks evenly.

4 Add tasty and colourful sauces and garnishes. For flavour use the juices that escape from the fish during steaming to make the sauce.

To give the fish eye-appeal as

well as flavour, counteract the whiteness of fish with colourful ingredients such as lemon or orange slices, tomatoes, mushrooms and strips of sweet pepper.

SUITABLE FISH FOR STEAMING

Steaming is primarily a method for cooking portions of fish or small whole fish, but it is not suitable for whole large fish. Use it for:
- thick fillets of round fish, cut in portions
- steaks or cutlets
- small whole white fish, such as dab or whiting
- thin fillets of flat fish which can either be folded or rolled.

FLAT FISH

All fish are hatched 'round' (as described on pages 1–20) with one eye on each side of the head. It is the habit of a flat fish to lie on the seabed, with the result that the eye that has no field of vision gradually works its way around towards the light to lie on the top side of the fish beside the other eye. The mouth, of course, remains in its original position. The body flattens to give the fish its characteristic shape. For camouflage the skin on the uppermost side becomes pigmented, but that on the underside remains pale. The skin on the unprotected side also becomes considerably thicker than that on the lower side.

The colour and marking of the dark skin varies considerably in tone, even within the same species, as this is nature's way of camouflaging the fish to make it as indistinguishable as possible from its natural background of pebbles, sand or mud. Which side of the fish becomes pigmented depends on the species, and results in some fish being known as 'right handed' and some as 'left handed'.

To decide the 'handedness' of a particular fish all you have to do is to hold it, dark side uppermost, with the gut cavity nearest to you. If the head then points to your left, the fish is left handed, and vice versa. In fact the only three left-handed fish commonly used for food in the United Kingdom are turbot, brill and megrim; the others are all right handed.

All flat fish are white fish (oily fish are all round). Flat fish only make up a small percentage of the white fish

landings but they include many different species of varying sizes. Depending on the catches, these fish are available all the year round, but are least plentiful, and not at their best, in spring, that is, during and immediately after spawning. For convenience the flat fish are divided into two groups.

Small flat fish include plaice and sole, the smaller specimens of which are often bought whole, while the larger ones can be bought either whole or filleted.

Large flat fish such as halibut and turbot, are usually cut up for sale by the fishmonger, but smaller specimens are sometimes sold whole. Sizes are very variable, depending on the age of the fish when caught.

CHOOSING FLAT FISH

Like round and oily fish, the sooner most flat fish are cooked after catching the better they taste. So look first for signs of freshness, for fish in season, and for small to medium-sized fish in preference to larger fish of the same species. Always look for plump, thick fish or fillets rather than thin ones. It is useful to know that the dark-skinned upper fillets of flat fish are usually thicker than those from the underside.

Whole fish. Look for a firm fish with bright, fresh colouring and a moist skin. Fish when just caught, and therefore very fresh, often has a positively slimy skin (especially lemon sole). This protects the fish from going stale, so do not wash it off until you are preparing the fish for cooking. Eyes should be bright and protruding, rather than dull and sunken. Dryness, floppiness or anything other than a clean, fresh smell are signs of staleness.

Fillets and cutlets. The flesh should have a bright, firm look. Avoid fish with a spongy texture or dull surface.

Frozen fish. Inshore fish (that·is, caught near the shore), frozen on landing, or fish frozen at sea, can be fresher than so called 'fresh fish' bought inland. Generally speaking, however, with the exception of plaice, flat fish are not available in sufficient quantities for mass-market freezing.

Buy frozen fish where the turnover is rapid, because once in the distribution chain the recommended storage life of frozen white fish is up to three months.

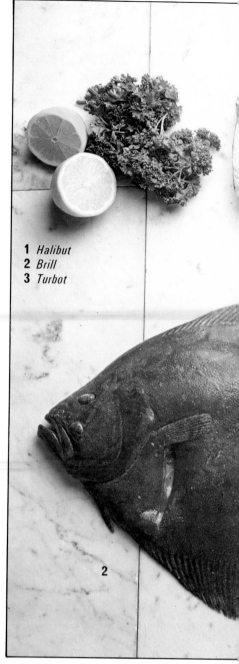

1 *Halibut*
2 *Brill*
3 *Turbot*

Large varieties of flat fish

TURBOT

Turbot is a thick, left-handed, round-shaped fish. The darker skin is a dull grey-brown with lighter specks and darker blotches and occasional blunt, boney tubercles. Turbot is a fine-flavoured, firm-fleshed fish and relatively expensive.

How sold: the fish is cut up into cutlets and fillets. Small, or chicken turbot, is sometimes sold for cooking

and serving whole.

Ways of cooking: cook cutlets by any method. Whole turbot is sometimes poached in a specially shaped fish kettle. Turbot is very good served cold.

Brill

Brill is very similar to turbot, but with a smooth skin and slightly more oval shape. The dark skin is fawnish-brown, the underside white with pinkish markings. Only small quantities of brill are landed. Brill is usually less expensive than turbot.

How sold: as for turbot.

Ways of cooking: as for turbot. Brill is particularly good grilled.

HALIBUT

A long, right-handed, diamond-shaped fish with thickish body. The dark skin is seen in varying shades of dark green to grey, the underside is white. Potentially halibut is the largest of the flat fish. Small, immature fish are known as chicken halibut. A choice, firm-fleshed and fine-flavoured fish, halibut is relatively expensive.

How sold: halibut is usually sold in cutlets cut right across the fish. These are cut in half if from very large fish. The tail piece is sold as one cut.

Ways of cooking: cook cutlets by any method. Halibut is a substantial and satisfying fish. The tail piece is usually poached or braised. A good

fish for serving cold.

MOCK HALIBUT (Greenland halibut, blue halibut)

This fish is rather similar to halibut but the dark skin is purple-brown and the underside is also pigmented. It is less expensive than true halibut but the flavour and texture are inferior to it.

How sold: rarely seen whole, this fish is usually cut into cutlets or fillets at the port and transported frozen.

Ways of cooking: cook this fish by any method, but good seasoning and sauces are needed to compensate for lack of flavour and texture.

1 Lemon sole
2 Dover sole
3 John Dory
4 Dab
5 Witch
6 Plaice

Small varieties of flat fish

PLAICE

This is a right-handed, 'pointed oval-shaped' fish. The tone colour of the dark skin is variable—speckled with many orange, red, yellow or chestnut spots—and also varies according to habitat. The underside is creamy white. This is a soft-textured fish with variable flavour.

How sold: small fish are sold whole or as cross-cut fillets, larger fish are sold whole or as quarter-cut fillets.

Ways of cooking: cook fillets by any method. Coating and frying helps to add crispness and texture. Plaice is best served with rich and tasty sauces.

DAB

Dab is a right-handed fish of ovoid shape. The dark skin is grey-brown with dark speckles (but no coloured spots), the underside is a broken white. This is an inshore fish, locally caught, with good landings off the English Channel. It can grow up to 42 cm [17"] long. Dab has a good flavour and firm texture.

How sold: usual landings of small fish, up to 350 g [¾ lb] are sold whole. The heads are usually left on but they can be removed if wished. Larger dab can be filleted.

Ways of cooking: dab is best cooked on the bone, whole, by grilling, frying or steaming. It can be cut crosswise into slices and fried. Fillets of dab can be cooked by any method.

FLOUNDER (fluke)

This is an ovoid fish, normally right handed (but can be found reversed). An inshore fish, it sometimes lives in fresh water inlets. The variable dark skin has reddish blotches, while the underside is opaque white. Landings of the fish are small.

How sold: flounder is usually sold whole, but if the fish is large enough the fishmonger will fillet it for you.

Ways of cooking: if caught in brackish water, the fish can have a muddy flavour which may be counteracted by sprinkling with salt and leaving overnight. Cook it by any method.

SOLE

Dover sole is considered the aristocrat of the sole family. It is a right-handed fish with a narrow streamlined shape. The upper side has dark grey blotched skin, with white underside. This firm-fleshed fish of fine flavour is expensive.

How sold: Dover sole: 225–700 g [½–1½ lb], slips: 175–225 g [6–8 oz], tongues: 100–175 g [4–6 oz]. Smaller fish are sold whole, but large fish of 450 g [1 lb] or over can be filleted. A whole fish usually has the head left on. It is usual to remove the dark skin only.

Ways of cooking: cook sole by any method. Small fish are best grilled, or fried à la meuniére, on the bone. Fillets are usually poached and used as the base for a vast range of classic fish dishes. Bones and trimmings should be used for making stock.

LEMON SOLE (smear dab)
A right-handed lemon-shaped plump fish. The darker side is a distinctive golden to sandy-brown colour with a creamy white underside. An excellent fish for eating, of fine flavour and medium-firm texture. In Scotland often referred to as 'sole'.

How sold: as for sole.
Ways of cooking: as for sole.

WITCH (Torbay sole, pole dab or grey sole)
A thin, right-handed fish of elongated oval shape. It is easily recognised by its almost transparent appearance and 'ragged' fins. The dark skin is mottled pale brown, the underside is greyish white. This is a cheaper fish of inferior quality and has a low yield of flesh to bones.

How sold: witch is usually sold whole, but could be filleted if it were large enough.
Ways of cooking: as for plaice.

MEGRIM (whiff, meg, Scarborough sole)
A thin, left-handed fish of oval shape. The dark skin is light brown in colour with yellow and dark brown blotches; the underside is off-white.

How sold: megrim is usually sold whole, but could be filleted if large enough.
Ways of cooking: as for plaice.

JOHN DORY
This distinctive fish is not strictly a flat fish, but a round fish flattened sideways with an eye on each side of the head. The colouring all over is olive to brown with yellowish wavy bands. Its distinguishing features are a large black mark (St Peter's thumb mark) in the centre and a large head. Small landings make this an expensive fish, but one of fine flavour and texture.

How sold: John Dory is sold whole if small (allow for beheading and trimming) or in quarter-cut fillets if large enough.
Ways of cooking: grill, steam, poach or fry.

25

Step-by-step to cross-cut fillets of flat fish

1 To prepare cross-cut fillets, lay fish on board with head facing you. Cut off head and tail. Trim fins.

2 Place the knife with blade facing away from you at the head end. Push knife under flesh.

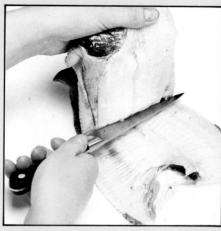

3 Work along backbone, and with a sawing movement work towards the outer edge to free fillet.

Step-by-step to skinning fillet of flat fish

1 To skin a fillet, lay the fillet with its skin down and tail end towards you.

2 About 12 mm [½"] from the tail end cut through the flesh down to the skin.

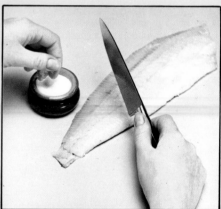

3 Hold the tail of the fish firmly with fingers dipped in salt and, with the other hand, hold the knife.

Step-by-step to skinning a Dover sole

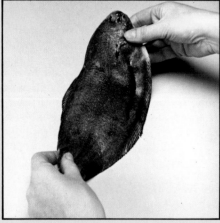

1 Place the fish with its dark skin facing upwards and tail end towards you.

2 Cut through the skin about 12 mm [½"] from the tail end and free enough skin to catch hold of.

3 Dip fingers in salt and hold the tail firmly with the one hand and grip skin with the other hand.

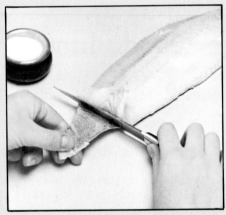

4 With the knife firmly against the skin, work the flesh up and away to free it completely.

4 With a swift movement rip the skin off from tail to head. It should come away in one piece.

The top-left panel:

4 Don't turn the fish over but repeat on the other side of the backbone to free second fillet.

Step-by-step to quarter-cut flat fish

1 To prepare quarter-cut fillets, lay fish, dark skin up, on a board. Cut off head and tail. Trim fins.

2 Place the fish with its tail end facing you. Cut down to the bone along the length of the fish.

3 To remove the first fillet, work the knife into the cut and gently lift the flesh.

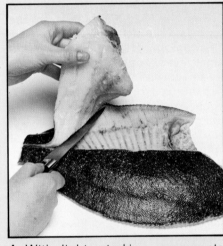

4 With light, stroking movements use the knife to free the fillet from the head end to the tail.

5 To remove the second fillet, turn the fish round and repeat the same action.

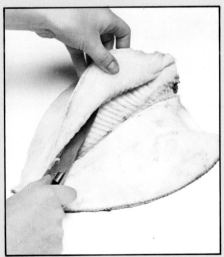

6 Turn the fish over so that the white skin is facing upwards. Remove two remaining fillets.

QUANTITIES

People's appetites vary enormously but, as a rough guide, any one of the following will provide enough for a main dish for one adult.

Fillets—150–175 g [5–6 oz].

Cutlets—175–200 g [6–7 oz]—slightly more than for fillets to allow for the bones.

One small whole fish—250–350 g [9–12 oz]. Additional weight here allows for head, tail and bones.

Large whole fish—allow 225 g [½ lb] per portion. This allows for the head and tail wastage. The weight of steaks or cutlets cut from large whole fish should be as given above.

PREPARING FLAT FISH FOR COOKING

Flat fish of not more than 450 g [1 lb] in weight is usually sold and cooked on the bone. To gut a flat fish make a semi-circular slit on the dark side behind the head and scrape out the entrails (flat fish have a relatively small amount of intestines). Fish with small heads, dabs for example, can be served with the head on, but if the fish has a large, unattractive head, such as John Dory, this must be removed. A good fishmonger will always fillet small flat fish for you without charge, and will also remove the skin if you wish. However, neither job is difficult to do yourself.

Cross-cut fillets. This means you get two fillets from each fish, one fillet taken right across the backbone on each side of the fish, making two good portions. This method is used for flat fish weighing 350–450 g [¾–1 lb]. Cross-cut fillets are naturally thin and are therefore not usually steamed.

Quarter-cut fillets. This method gives you four fillets from a fish, one fillet from either side of the backbone and two fillets from each side of the fish. This is the usual method for flat fish weighing 450–900 g [1–2 lb]. Quarter-cut fillets can be skinned or not according to preference. Often only the dark-skinned fillets, which are naturally thicker, are skinned.

STEAMING FISH

Keeping fish is not recommended. Generally fish should be cooked on the day of purchase and it should never be kept for longer than 24 hours.

Ideally, the fish should be pre-pared as close to cooking time as possible. However, this is not always convenient and if preparation is done a few hours in advance no harm will be done. Cover the fish when prepared and keep it chilled until it is required for cooking.

If the fish is to be steamed, it can be prepared as soon as you get it home. Skin and fillet the fish if you wish, season it with salt and pepper and a squeeze of lemon juice. It is a positive advantage to season fish a little ahead of cooking it, and not only when steaming. Then cover and refrigerate it until it is time to start cooking. If other seasonings and flavourings, such as soy sauce, are used, add these just before cooking.

Steaming is a method whereby fish is cooked in the vapour of boiling water. Fish should always be steamed by the closed method. This ensures that all the nutrients and flavour are preserved, either in the fish itself or in the juices which escape from the fish into the container. These juices can then be added to the sauce. This way all the food value and flavour is retained and nothing is lost.

The rate of cooking is fairly rapid, although slower than when fish is poached or cooked in an open steamer. Naturally it helps to speed things if a good heat conductor, such as an aluminium container, is used rather than one of thick china.

Equipment for steaming

There are many different types of steamer available but for fish the container must be a suitable size for the type of fish being steamed. Because fish should always be cooked in a closed steamer, it is often parcelled in foil or greaseproof paper and cooked in one of the improvised steamers.

Small pieces of fish, steaks and cutlets can be steamed on a plate covered with foil or sandwiched between two plates, in either case placed over a saucepan of boiling water. Soup plates, being slightly domed, are a good shape, although aluminium or enamelled plates are better heat conductors.

Large pieces of fish, rolled or folded fillets and small whole fish are securely parcelled in foil or grease-proof paper and placed in a tiered steamer, flower-shaped steamer, two-handled metal colander or a Chinese tiered steamer. This stands in the container and the water should not reach to the level of the parcel. (The only exception to this is when a fish kettle is used; this does not use the closed method of steaming and is covered in a later course.)

The saucepan is then covered with a well-fitting lid or, when a colander is used, a sheet of foil may provide a more effective seal.

Points for successful steaming

Whatever type of steamer is used, observe the following points.

● Ensure that the container of fish does not touch the water but is completely surrounded by freely circulating steam.

● Cover the steamer really tightly with a well-fitting lid or foil, so that no steam can escape while cooking is in progress.

● Lightly grease the grid or foil in which the fish rests just sufficiently to prevent the fish sticking (fish skin tends to stick readily).

Handy hints

A good sauce is the perfect complement to fish. The more modest the fish and the plainer the method of cooking, the more important the sauce becomes, for adding both richness and flavour.

● White sauces such as béchamel and velouté are both ideal accompaniments to fish.

● From among the béchamel-based sauces there are complementary flavours, choose from anchovy, cheese, egg, Mornay, mushroom, parsley and prawn. For oily fish choose a mustard sauce.

● For richer sauces serve a velouté-based sauce. Choose from Bercy, Chivry, mushroom and polonaise.

● Save fuel by cooking vegetables which are to be served at the same meal in the same saucepan under the fish steamer. Boil the vegetables, such as potatoes, by placing them directly in the water in the bottom of the steamer pan. Alternatively, steam them by placing them in foil parcels on another tiered steamer above the water and the fish. Serve the vegetables with the fish.

Step-by-step to steaming fish

1 If steaming on a plate grease it lightly to prevent the fish sticking to it.

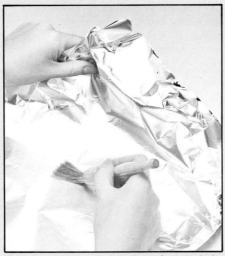

OR if steaming in kitchen foil, lightly grease a piece large enough in which to wrap the fish securely.

2 Place fish on plate or foil in a single layer. Season well with salt, white pepper and lemon juice.

3 Cover the fish with another plate or with kitchen foil and refrigerate it until required for cooking.

4 Prepare a steamer and bring the water to the boil. The water must not touch the fish container.

5 Add any other seasoning or flavouring, such as soy sauce, to the fish parcel.

6 To steam the fish on the plate make sure that it is well covered. Place it over pan to cook.

OR to steam fish in foil make sure foil is secure and place on the steamer to cook. Cover pan.

7 Remove fish from steamer to serve and add cooking juices to accompanying sauce.

● Wait until the water is boiling and steam is rising before starting to cook the fish.

● Keep the water boiling. It is not usually necessary to top up with additional boiling water during cooking because fish steams quickly.

● Do not overcook the fish, as this affects the flavour and texture of the fish.

Steaming times

Fish cooks extremely quickly and it is all too easy to overcook. It would be a pity to do this as the fish loses its delicate flavour.

Steaming times differ, depending on the size of the fish, its container and the method of steaming. For example, fish steamed on a china plate will take slightly longer than fish steamed in greaseproof paper or in an aluminium or enamelled plate. A china plate can, of course, be heated before adding the fish but this is not always convenient.

Depending on the container small pieces of fish, such as thin fillets, will take about 8–15 minutes; thicker fillets, folded or rolled, will take 15–25 minutes. The longest time fish should be steamed is 25 minutes. A 2.5 cm [1"] thick cutlet or steak may well take 20 minutes, but always check towards the end of cooking time to make sure that the fish is not being overcooked.

Fish is cooked when the flesh becomes opaque and comes away from the bone. In the case of very fresh fish a white creamy substance oozes from between the flakes.

COOKING FISH TO SERVE COLD

Cold fish dishes can be most attractive to look at and delicious to eat. Colourful fish salads with creamy dressings make light and refreshing main dishes, while smaller portions of fish with piquant dressings make excellent first courses. The latter include simple pickled and soused fish (described on pages 61–67).

The very best white fish for serving cold are the more expensive ones, such as turbot and halibut. These can be served fairly plainly (as is shown in the star recipe). Excellent dishes can, however, be made from cheaper fish, provided you dress them up with sharp-flavoured creamy dressings and colourful garnishes. Use a sauce that is not only piquant but also colourful.

Steaming is a good way of cooking white fish for salads because there is no loss of nutrients or flavour. For serving cold the important point to remember is not to cook too far in advance. When cold, the sooner the fish is eaten the moister and tastier it will be.

Smoked whole fish for serving cold or reheating is probably better poached in milk and water. This method takes care of any excess saltiness.

When oily fish is to be served cold, it is best to grill, pickle or souse it. (Poaching and sousing are described on pages 41–51 and 61–67. For grilling oily fish see on pages 11–20.)

STEAMED FILLETS WITH CHIVE AND CUCUMBER SAUCE

These fillets of flat fish are cooked on a plate, covered with foil and set over a saucepan of simmering water. This is a very convenient method when cooking for 2 to 4 people only. It is also a very economical way of cooking, especially if you cook vegetables in the water beneath the fish. Any variety of small flat fish fillets can be used, but naturally the better the fish the better the dish. Unless it is being cooked for invalids, steamed fish is best served with a rich, well-flavoured sauce. This is especially true of the less interesting varieties of flat fish. If fresh chives are not available, use chopped spring onions, but sweat and then cook them with cucumber.

SERVES 4
**4 flat fish fillets, about 150 g [5 oz] each
salt and white pepper
half a lemon
half a small cucumber
50 g [2 oz] butter
25 g [1 oz] flour
250 ml [½ pt] milk
30 ml [2 tablespoons] chopped fresh chives**

1 Select a large, heatproof plate (aluminium is best) which is large enough to hold the fish in a single layer and will rest on the top of a large saucepan. Grease it very lightly with butter. Then butter a piece of greaseproof paper or foil large enough to cover it completely.

2 If the fishmonger has not already done so, skin any dark-skinned fillets.

3 Lay the fillets flat on the greased plate, putting unskinned fillets skin side up. Sprinkle well with salt and a little white pepper. Squeeze the lemon and add the juice.

4 Fold each fillet in three. Cover the plate with the greased covering. Secure the parcel firmly and refrigerate until ready to cook.

5 Half fill a saucepan with water and bring to boiling point. Set the covered plate on top and cover with the lid of the pan, being careful not to perforate the covering.

6 Steam for 10–15 minutes, depending on the thickness of the fillets.

7 While the fish is cooking, prepare the sauce. Wipe the cucumber and chop it roughly into very small dice.

8 Melt 25 g [1 oz] butter in a small heavy-based saucepan, put in the cucumber, stir well, cover and leave to sweat over low heat for 5 minutes.

9 Melt the remaining butter in another small saucepan. Add the flour off the heat and cook, stirring, over low heat for 1 minute to make a roux.

10 Off the heat blend in the milk smoothly, then return to the heat and stir until boiling. Cover and leave to simmer over low heat.

11 Check the fish; when cooked the fillets will look opaque. Transfer the cooked fillets with a fish slice to a hot serving dish and keep warm.

12 Stir the fish juices which have collected in the plate into the sauce. Add the cucumber, chives and seasoning to taste.

13 Stir and simmer for a moment or two then pour over the fish.

Steamed mackerel fillets served with a piquant sauce flavoured with capers, mustard and chopped parsley.

CHINESE STEAMED FISH

This makes a light main course for two people. Instead of the fillets of plaice you can use a whole dab weighing 700 g [1½ lb] or two whiting each weighing 250–350 g [9–12 oz].

If you have some white wine you can use it instead of the wine vinegar, in which case omit the sugar. Steamed rice and green beans are a suitable accompaniment.

SERVES 2
2 plaice fillets weighing about 175 g [6 oz] each
100 g [¼ lb] mushrooms
1 garlic clove
2 spring onions, finely chopped or 30 ml [2 tablespoons] chopped onions or shallots
5 ml [1 teaspoon] cornflour
30 ml [2 tablespoons] soy sauce
60 ml [4 tablespoons] sesame oil
15 ml [1 tablespoon] wine vinegar
1.5 ml [¼ teaspoon] sugar
salt and pepper

1 Select a plate large enough to hold the fish in a single layer and grease it lightly.

2 Place the fish on the plate and season. Slice the mushrooms very thinly and add to fish.

3 Peel and finely chop the garlic and add it to the finely chopped onions in a small mixing bowl.

4 Blend the cornflour with the soy sauce and add to the onions. Stir in the oil, vinegar, sugar and some pepper. Mix well.

5 Add to the fish. Cover securely with another lightly greased plate or foil.

6 Steam for 10–15 minutes. Serve immediately.

MACKEREL FILLETS WITH PIQUANT SAUCE

Oily fish, such as herring and mackerel, can be steamed too. Gutted whole fish can be wrapped in greaseproof paper or kitchen foil and steamed, or fillets can be steamed flat or rolled. For mustard sauce, mix 5 ml [1 teaspoon] each of English mustard, white wine vinegar and caster sugar into 250 ml [½ pint] basic white sauce. Oily fish for successful steaming must be fresh. If you cannot buy mackerel large enough for this recipe, buy four small ones instead. The steaming time here is slightly longer because the fillets are folded.

SERVES 4
2 mackerel, weighing about 500 g [18 oz] each
salt and pepper
15 ml [1 tablespoon] lemon juice

For the sauce:
250 ml [½ pt] mustard sauce
10 ml [2 teaspoons] capers
10 ml [2 teaspoons] freshly chopped parsley

For the garnish:
2 tomatoes
bunch of watercress

1 Wash and fillet the mackerel (see pages 4–5).

2 Lay the fillets on a piece of oiled greaseproof paper or kitchen foil. Sprinkle with plenty of salt, a little pepper and some lemon juice.

3 Fold each fillet into three.

4 Wrap the fish into a secure parcel.

5 Prepare the steamer and place the parcel over the boiling water. Steam for 20–25 minutes, depending on the size of the fillets.

6 Meanwhile prepare the sauce and let it simmer gently until the fish is cooked.

7 Transfer the fish on to a serving dish. Add the fish juices to the sauce. Crush the capers and add to the sauce with the parsley. Pour over the fish.

8 Garnish with tomato wedges and sprigs of watercress. Serve immediately.

Right out of water

Baking is one of the easiest ways to cook fish and often the best. Whole fish, steaks and fillets can all be cooked in this way. Since you cook them with little or no liquid except their own juices, none of their flavour or nutrients seep away. Baking is also a very good way to cook stuffed fish.

The term baking fish covers several simple methods of cooking fish in the oven. The amount of liquid or fat that is used is always small and this distinguishes baking from other oven-cooking processes, such as casseroling, braising and sousing. Liquid and/or fat are added to help keep the fish moist while it is cooking. These prevent it sticking to the dish and add extra flavour.

Baking is a very adaptable and trouble-free way to cook fish. No matter the shape, your fish will remain firm and appetizing. Even fish which breaks or flakes easily can be baked successfully as you can serve it straight from the dish in which it has been cooked. This saves on the washing up too!

There are five methods of baking fish: sur le plat, en papillote, au gratin, with a savoury topping and roasting. The first two methods, which are the simplest, are suitable for all varieties of fish. A gratin or savoury topping can be used with any fish except for a whole round fish (which can be egg and breadcrumbed instead). The roasting method is generally used for larger varieties of round fish which are to be cooked whole.

All the methods apply the principle of a minimum of added liquid or fat and with each method the fish is cooked in its natural juices, so all its flavour and goodness are contained. With a quality fish of fine flavour, the addition of a few herbs will be sufficient to bring the flavour out to the full. With a more modest fish the tasty coatings and stuffings which can be used will compensate for flavour which the fish may lack.

A fish can be baked, stuffed, as easily as it can be baked plain. The fish is cooked in exactly the same way, but for slightly longer if the fish is stuffed; the stuffing provides extra flavour and ekes out the fish.

When baking fish, a variety of effects can be achieved. The presentation can be impressive while little time-consuming effort is demanded of the cook.

EQUIPMENT

A baking dish and foil are all that are required in the way of cooking apparatus, though you will need the usual equipment for preparing the fish (listed on page 4) and also bowls and other equipment for preparing any stuffings.

Fish bricks

The one specialized piece of equipment you may come across and wish to use is the fish brick. This is designed to take round fish, fillets or portions, but not whole flat fish. The brick is prepared by lining the bottom with oiled or buttered greaseproof paper or foil. This makes the cleaning of the brick easier, as it can be scrubbed, but no detergent must be used in the water. The brick would absorb and hold the soapy flavour and the perfumed smell.

Unlike chicken bricks, a fish brick does not need to be soaked in water before use. It should, though, always be placed in a cold oven. The oven is then set at the required temperature. Small fish should be cooked at a high temperature, 230°C [450°F] gas mark 8 and will need about 25-30 minutes, timed from the minute the brick is placed in the oven. Larger fish or portions of fish require slower cooking at 180°C [350°F] gas mark 4. A fish or portion of fish weighing about 1.1 – 1.4 kg [2½–3 lb] will need an hour and

maybe longer at this temperature, depending on the thickness of the fish. Remember to allow a slightly longer cooking time (about 10 minutes) if cooking stuffed fish, to allow the heat to penetrate right through the stuffing.

PREPARING YOUR FISH

Fish does not keep well. It should be bought as fresh as possible and should preferably be cooked on the day it is bought. It should never be kept longer than 24 hours. Having bought your fish, unwrap it, rinse it under cold running water and drain it thoroughly.

Ideally, the fish should be prepared just before cooking but if this is not convenient no harm will be done if the preparation is undertaken a few hours beforehand. In fact, it is a positive advantage to be able to season the fish a little in advance as it helps the flavour. Keep the prepared fish covered and refrigerate.

If a fish is bought whole it must be scaled and gutted. Clean (scale and gut) the fish and fillet it if this is how you intend to serve it. These processes are fully discussed for round fish on page 4 and for flat fish on page 28. Reserve the roe and liver for possible use in the stuffing. Season the flesh with salt and pepper and a squeeze of lemon juice. The removal of the head and tail from the whole fish is a matter of personal preference, as is the skinning of a whole fish or fillets. A large expanse of dark skin on a flat fish or fillet can look very unappetizing to some people and can be quickly removed (see pages 26–27).

If you want to stuff a fish and bake it whole, the removal of the backbone will create a large cavity and make eating easier. However, this is optional, and is only possible with round fish (see pages 4–5).

OVEN TEMPERATURE AND TIMING

Once in the oven fish needs so little attention that it is easy to leave it there too long. If you are busy you may be tempted to think that a few moments' extra cooking will not matter; don't be misled. Fish cooks remarkably quickly in comparison to meat and once overcooked cannot be rescued. It may dry out and will then have a 'flannelly' texture, despite any

flavouring, wine or butter you may have added. It may be completely ruined and you will have wasted both time and money.

As a rule the oven temperature when baking fish is moderate: 180-190°C [350-375°F] gas mark 4-5. A higher temperature is needed initially for the roasting method, 230°C [450°F] gas mark 8, which is then reduced to 160°C [325°F] gas mark 3. When browning a gratin, the temperature will be raised during the last few minutes of cooking to 230°C [450°F] gas mark 8.

One cannot set fixed times for baking fish. Exact times vary according to the size and thickness of the fish, on whether it is fresh or frozen and on whether it is cooked plain or stuffed. Use the times given as a general guide only for baking fresh fish. (Allow slightly longer for frozen fish.)

Bake thin fillets for 8-12 minutes and for up to 20 minutes if stuffed. Bake thick fillets, steaks, cutlets and small whole fish for 15-20 minutes and for up to 30 minutes if stuffed. Bake whole large fish for 25-30 minutes and for up to 45 minutes if stuffed.

Testing for readiness

Baked fish is cooked when it is opaque right through and the fish comes away easily from the bone. The easiest way of testing to see if it is cooked is to pierce the thickest part of the fish with a thin skewer. The skewer will go in and come out without any resistance when the fish is cooked. It is advisable to test the fish before the recommended cooking time is quite completed. The fish can always be returned to the oven if it is not cooked, but overcooking cannot be remedied.

SUR LE PLAT

This method of baking is the simplest and most straightforward. It is suitable for whole flat fish, fillets, steaks and cutlets. Being a plain dish it is most important that the fish is absolutely fresh and that fine-flavoured ingredients are used. The fish that is classically associated with this method of baking is sole, but many other varieties of white fish, such as plaice, lemon sole and whiting, are perfectly acceptable.

Although margarine can be substituted for butter in many recipes,

the simplicity of this baking method makes it desirable to use butter.

Prepare the fish and season with salt and pepper and a squeeze of lemon juice. A whole fish should be skinned for this recipe but the removal of the head and tail is optional. Dark-skinned fillets may be skinned if preferred.

Choose a shallow, flameproof dish into which the fish will fit snugly in one layer. The dish needs to be flameproof as the cooking is finished off under a hot grill. Butter the dish well and lay the fish in it. Place thin fillets slightly overlapping each other. Pour in a very little liquid, not more than 15 ml [1 tablespoon] for four small fillets or 60 ml [4 tablespoons] for a whole fish weighing 900 g [2 lb]. Dry white wine or strong fish stock is frequently used but dry vermouth is very successful as only a small quantity is needed. Dry cider, thin cream or top of the milk can also be used. Dot the fish all over with a little butter (in small dabs) and cover the dish securely but not tightly with buttered greaseproof paper or foil. Bake at 180°C [350°F] gas mark 4 until the fish is tender.

Basting during cooking is not necessary as the dish is closely covered and all the juices are contained. When the cooking time is almost completed, turn on the grill to hot and test the fish to see if it is baked.

When the fish is cooked right through, remove the paper cover and baste the fish with some of the buttery juice. Pop the dish under the hot grill for a couple of minutes (no longer) to glaze the fish lightly.

If you wish to serve the fish cold, replace any butter in the recipe with oil. It is unnecessary to glaze a fish to be chilled after baking. Simply remove it from the oven; place the fish in a cold serving dish, cover loosely and allow to become cold. Then keep it chilled. Do make sure that there is sufficient liquid in the dish to keep it moist. The fish should be eaten on the day it is cooked.

EN PAPILLOTE

Cooking 'en papillote' means, literally in a paper case. Fish is wrapped in greased foil with fat, liquids and flavourings, then baked. Greaseproof paper can be used but it is harder to seal.

The main advantage of cooking en

The cleanest, and a very simple way to bake whole fish, fillets and steaks is in foil parcels.

papillote is that the added flavourings are easily adapted to suit the fish (and your purse) and are firmly sealed in with each parcel. There need be no fear of lost goodness or watering down of flavour, while this must surely be the cleanest way of cooking. The juices, being sealed in, do not even dirty the baking tray on which the parcels are cooked and these can be transferred unopened, directly on to plates.

This method of cooking is suitable for small whole fish; thick fillets, steaks and cutlets. Prepare the whole fish by cleaning and seasoning with salt and pepper and a squeeze of lemon juice. The skinning of the dark side of a flat fish is a matter of personal preference but the head and tail should not be removed. Dark-skinned fillets can be skinned, if preferred.

Select your flavouring ingredients to suit your fish. A fine-flavoured fish can be treated simply (as sur le plat) while a cheaper, less flavoursome fish can be stuffed before cooking and/or be baked with a savoury topping.

Using savoury butters
Savoury butters, placed on the fish, will keep it moist during cooking and also improve the flavour. You will need about 50 g [2 oz] butter for four parcels.

Here are some ideas particularly suited to fish.

To make all the following butters start by mashing 50 g [2 oz] unsalted butter.
● To make anchovy butter add 3-4 crushed anchovies.
● For aniseed butter add 10-15 ml [2-3 teaspoons] Pernod, pastis or Ricard.
● For mustard butter add 10 ml [2 teaspoons] French mustard and a seasoning of salt and pepper.
● For orange butter add 10 ml [2 teaspoons] each of orange juice and grated zest.

The butters can be used with any species of fish but mustard butter and aniseed butter go particularly well with oily fish.

Making the case
The paper case for the fish could not be easier to make. It can, in fact, be made of greaseproof paper or aluminium foil. Foil is easier to handle as it is more malleable and forms a better seal when the edges are crimped together.

Cut a double thickness of foil or paper large enough to enclose the fish generously. Grease the foil or paper with melted butter if you intend eating the fish hot, or with oil if you plan to eat it cold. Season it lightly.

Wrapping the fish
Place a piece of prepared foil or paper on a baking tray. Place the fish in the centre and add the flavourings. Pull up the edges of the foil or paper and twist them together over the fish to make a baggy parcel. Crimp the ends together firmly too. Continue with the other pieces of fish and then place the baking tray in the oven. Bake the fish at 190°C [375°F] gas mark 5 until tender.

Serving the fish
To serve the parcels in style, open up the edges and fold them back to display the top of the fish. You can pinch or snip the edges into shapes such as petals and garnish each parcel with parsley or watercress.

If you wish to serve the fish cold, it must be removed from the foil (where it would continue to cook gently). Keep the fish moist and chilled and eat it the day it is cooked.

AU GRATIN
Gratin is the term given to the thin crust which forms on a dish which is 'browned on top'. The gratin is made by sprinkling the dish with fresh breadcrumbs, grated cheese or with a mixture of breadcrumbs and flavouring ingredients such as herbs, spices or cheese. You will need about 50 g [2 oz] gratin for a dish for four people. A gratin can be used to coat a whole flat fish, steaks and fillets and pieces of fish on top. Whole fish is more successfully treated by rolling in egg and breadcrumbs before baking.

Cooking the gratin with the fish
Clean the fish as usual and skin it; the head and tail may be removed if preferred. Season with salt and pepper and a squeeze of lemon juice. Butter a shallow dish and place the fish in it, either with extra butter, with a little liquid or in a coating sauce. Cover the surface with the gratin and dot with flakes of softened butter. Bake uncovered, in order that the gratin may brown, at 190°C [375°F] gas mark 5. If the gratin is not

sufficiently browned by the time the fish is cooked, either raise the temperature of the oven to 230°C [450°F] gas mark 8 for 2-3 minutes, or place the dish under a hot grill to get the same results.

Adding the gratin after cooking
If you are adding the gratin to a cooked dish, bake the fish, either sur le plat or with a coating sauce or savoury topping (see below). Add the uncooked crumbs, cheese and any other ingredients and pop into the hot oven for 2-3 minutes. Alternatively, sprinkle ready-fried or toasted crumbs over the dish and serve straight away. Bread that is a few days old and less moist is best for making breadcrumbs. Dark rye breadcrumbs in place of white add a bite to fish.

SAVOURY TOPPINGS
This is a particularly good method for baking the less glamorous types of fish. An added bonus—and one of the stimulating features of baking—is that you can completely change the flavour simply by changing the topping.

The method is suitable for all fish except whole round fish. The topping is added in the same way as a gratin, but in this case the topping is made from soft ingredients and is not browned.

Preparing the fish
Clean the fish and season it with salt and pepper and a squeeze of lemon. Remove the head and tail from the whole fish and skin it, or use skinned fillets if preferred. Butter an oven-proof dish well and lay the prepared fish in it.

Adding the topping
The quantity of topping needed is about 50 ml [2 fl oz] for portions for four people. Mix the topping and then spoon it over the dish, dividing it between the fish or portions of fish. Cover the dish securely but not tightly with buttered greaseproof paper or foil. Bake the fish at 190°C [375°F] gas mark 5 until tender. Remove the covering and serve straight from the dish.

If serving cold, remove the fish and the topping to a cold serving dish. Cover and keep chilled. Eat the day it is cooked.

Suitable toppings

● For a cheesy cream topping mix 25 g [1 oz] grated Cheddar cheese and 5 ml [1 teaspoon] French mustard or 1.5 ml [¼ teaspoon] dry English mustard with 50 ml [2 fl oz] thick cream.

● For a crème fraiche topping add 25 ml [1 fl oz] sour cream to 50 ml [2 fl oz] thick cream.

● For a caper topping add 10 ml [2 teaspoons] capers to the crème fraiche.

● For a tomato cream add 5 ml [1 teaspoon] tomato purée and 1.5 ml [¼ teaspoon] dried basil to 50 ml [2 fl oz] thick cream.

● For a mushroom cream topping fry 100 g [¼ lb] mushrooms in a little butter, add the juice of a lemon to the pan, season with salt and pepper and turn the lemony mushrooms into 50 ml [2 fl oz] thick cream.

Two quick, easy toppings using readily available commercial products are:

● a small tin of condensed soup such as mushroom or tomato, well flavoured with herbs.

● a jar of cheese- or fish-flavoured baby food, well seasoned with salt and pepper; a 100 g [¼ lb] jar will serve four people, a 175 g [6 oz] jar will serve six people.

Stuffing a flat fish is a simple process. Slit the fish down the backbone, lift the flesh and spoon in the prepared stuffing.

ROASTING

This open cooking method of baking is ideal for larger varieties of fish which will not fit comfortably under a grill, such as sea bass, grey mullet, large red mullet and hake.

Preparing the fish

Scale and clean the fish and season the belly cavity with salt and pepper and a squeeze of lemon juice. Do not skin the fish but slash or slit the skin with a knife at 2.5 cm [1"] intervals on both sides. This prevents the skin splitting under the fierce heat and allows the heat to penetrate for even cooking. Brush the fish all over with a little olive oil and place it on a grid in a baking dish. The fish should be roasted at 230°C [450°F] gas mark 8 for five minutes, turning once, to allow the skin to crisp. The heat is then reduced to 160°C [325°F] gas mark 3 to allow the fish to cook in its thickest part. The fish should be turned once during the slow cooking and basted frequently with olive oil. When it is cooked, place the fish in a serving dish on a bed of watercress and serve

with wedges of lemon and a savoury butter.

STUFFING A FISH

Whole fish and fillets are as easy to bake with a stuffing as they are without one. Just remember to allow a little extra cooking time (about 10 minutes) to let the heat penetrate right through the stuffing.

If serving baked fish cold, it is advisable to make the stuffing on the moist side and to reduce any strongly flavoured ingredients, such as onion, to a minimum.

Round fish

You can stuff a round fish either in the cleaned belly cavity or you can remove the backbone and stuff the fish down its entire length. Removing the backbone is optional but it does give extra room so that you can use more stuffing. The fish is also easier to eat without the bones. The preparation and boning of a round fish is fully discussed on pages 4–5. Removing the head and tail is a matter of choice. When cleaning the fish reserve the liver and roe for possible use in the stuffing.

Make sure the cavity is quite clean by washing it under cold running water and remove any traces of blood

with salt. Season the inside of the fish with salt and pepper and a squeeze of lemon juice. Prepare your stuffing and stuff the fish, leaving room for the stuffing to swell. It may be necessary to stitch the opening together to contain the stuffing. Using strong thread (not nylon) and a large needle, oversew the edges with large stitches, or secure them with very small poultry skewers.

The fish may be baked lying on its side or upright with the cavity slit underneath. A round fish looks more dramatic upright, particularly when served this way, garnished with wedges of tomato and lemon and sprigs of parsley or watercress.

A smaller round fish can be prepared and boned, and rolled round the stuffing. Follow the directions for boning on pages 4–5 and remove the tail. Removing the head is optional. Spread the chosen stuffing all over the cut side, pressing it down if crumbly. Starting at the tail end, roll the fish up like a swiss roll. Secure the end with a couple of cocktail sticks or small poultry skewers. If the resulting roll is rather bulky and likely to be insecure, tie the roll with loops of fine string to prevent it unrolling. If you use string this limits you to baking the fish either sur le plat or en papillote

because it must be removed before serving. Cocktail sticks or skewers can be picked out fairly easily and you could bake fish, thus secured, with a savoury topping or egg and bread-crumbed.

Flat fish
Clean the fish as described on pages 26–27 and skin the dark side. Season it with salt and pepper and a squeeze of lemon. Place the fish on a board, skinned side up and make a slit with a knife along the length of the fish down the backbone. Work the knife into the cut and ease the flesh away from the bone, making a pocket between the flesh and the bone on each side. Season the inside of the pockets lightly with salt and pepper and a squeeze of lemon juice. Stuff the pockets loosely. The stuffing will swell; it will lift the flesh of the pocket making the fish look fatter, and will show as a line down the centre of the fish. If you do not object to the dark skin, lay the fish light side up and stuff without skinning.

Bake this stuffed fish either sur le plat or en papillote.

Fillets
Stuffing fish fillets is a good way to make them go further, especially thin ones. The stuffing can be done in any of the following ways.

Skin the fillets if preferred, season with salt and pepper and a squeeze of lemon juice and lay flat on a board (skinned side up if not skinned on both sides). Spread the surface of the fillet with the prepared stuffing and lay a second fillet (skinned side down) on top, making a sandwich.

Alternatively, having spread the fillet with the stuffing, roll it up, starting with the tail, and secure with a cocktail stick. A fillet roll can also be made by moulding the stuffing into little sausages and wrapping the fillet around. Again, start with the tail and secure the completed roll with a cocktail stick. These fillets can be baked sur le plat, en papillote, au gratin or with a savoury topping.

BASIC STUFFING
This standard basic stuffing is a good 'extender' to use with any fish (or with meat or poultry). You can fill it into the belly cavity of a large fish, or spread it over a flat fillet and then roll the fish up round it. You can layer it between small fish fillets, or roll it into

small balls and bake them with the fish, to garnish it. Assemble all the ingredients before starting the stuffing.

MAKES 200 G [7 OZ] STUFFING
1 lemon
100 g [¼ lb] fresh white breadcrumbs
50 g [2 oz] soft butter or margarine
15 ml [1 tablespoon] chopped parsley
2.5 ml [½ teaspoon] dried chopped mixed herbs
salt and pepper
pinch of grated or ground nutmeg
1 large egg

1 Grate the zest from the lemon. (The fruit and juice are not used.)

2 In a bowl, mix together all the ingredients except the egg.

3 In a small bowl, beat the egg and then add it to the other ingredients. Work it in until the mixture holds together lightly; it should not be a clogged mass. Check the seasoning.

Variations
● For ham stuffing, add 50 g [2 oz] minced cooked ham and a good pinch of ground allspice to the dry ingredients, and beat the egg with 30 ml [2 tablespoons] milk. Use for stuffing large coarse white fish.
● For orange stuffing, add 15 ml [1 tablespoon] grated orange zest plus 5 ml [1 teaspoon] grated lemon zest to the basic stuffing. Beat the egg with 10 ml [2 teaspoons] orange juice before mixing it in. Use the stuffing for whole sole or plaice, or for white fish fillets.
● For roe stuffing, poach 1-2 hard or soft roes from small fish in a very little salted water for 2-3 minutes. Chop them finely and add to the dry ingredients for the basic stuffing. Use this for any fish.
● For fresh mushroom stuffing, chop 100 g [¼ lb] mushrooms finely. Remove the rind from 50 g [2 oz] bacon, then chop the bacon and fry it for 2 minutes. Add the mushrooms and fry for 3 minutes. Mix the bacon, mushrooms and any fat in the pan with 100 g [¼ lb] fresh white breadcrumbs, 15 ml [1 tablespoon] softened butter, seasoning and a little grated nutmeg. Bind with 1 beaten egg. Use this to stuff any fish.

FILLETS OF SOLE BERCY

*This is an example of the sur le plat
method, the simplest and the classic
way to bake and serve whole flat fish or
fish fillets, especially sole. But lemon
sole, plaice or whiting fillets may also
be used. The flesh of these fish flakes
easily, so they are best left in the baking
dish and finished under the grill.*

SERVES 4
   **8 fillets of sole weighing in
      total about 700 g [1½ lb]
   salt and white pepper
   half a lemon
   30 ml [2 tablespoons] butter
   ½ shallot or 3 spring onions
   15 ml [1 tablespoon] chopped
      parsley
   60 ml [4 tablespoons] dry white
      wine or dry cider**

1 Heat the oven to 180°C [350°F] gas
   mark 4.

2 Skin the fillets if preferred. Free the
   flesh from the skin with the blunt
   side of the knife and, holding the
   skin firmly, rip it off. Pat the fillets
   dry with kitchen paper. Season on
   both sides with salt, pepper and a
   squeeze of lemon juice.

3 Take 15 ml [1 tablespoon] of the
   butter and grease a shallow flame-
   proof dish which will just hold the
   fillets in one layer, and a piece of
   greaseproof paper or foil large
   enough to cover the dish.

4 Chop the onion finely and scatter
   over the bottom of the dish with
   the chopped parsley. Lay the fillets
   on top in one layer, slightly
   overlapping them, and pour the
   cider or white wine over.

5 Dot the fillets with the remaining
   15 ml [1 tablespoon] butter. Cover
   the dish securely but not tightly
   with buttered greaseproof paper
   or foil.

6 Bake the fillets for 8-12 minutes,
   depending on their thickness.
   They should be milky white and
   tender when pierced with a thin
   skewer. While they are cooking,
   heat the grill to high.

7 Spoon some of the onion and the
   buttery liquid over the cooked
   fillets.

8 Place the dish under the grill for 2

minutes to glaze the fillets lightly.
Serve immediately, from the baking dish.

MACKEREL 'EN PAPILLOTE'

*Use this recipe as a model when you
cook any small whole fish, steaks or
fillets in parcels. Serve the packages
still closed, or with just the tops
unfolded, each with its juices still
sealed in it. Serve lemon wedges with
the parcels, and place a spare plate on
the table for the unwrapped foil or
paper*

SERVES 4
   **4 mackerel each weighing
      225-275 g [½-¾ lb]
   salt and pepper
   half a lemon
   1 small onion
   75 g [3 oz] butter
   15 ml [1 tablespoon] chopped
      parsley**

1 Heat the oven to 190°C [375°F] gas
   mark 5. Cut off the fins and tails of
   the fish but leave on the heads. Slit
   open the fish along the belly cavity,
   clean and rinse the fish. Pat dry.

2 Squeeze the lemon and season the

A haddock, stuffed with some home-made stuffing and coated with rye breadcrumbs, makes a dinner party dish. Garnish with colourful vegetables.

fish with salt and pepper and a little of the lemon juice.

3 Peel and chop the onion roughly.

4 Cream 50 g [2 oz] butter in a bowl. Mix in the onion, parsley, the remaining lemon juice, salt and a pinch of pepper.

5 Divide the mixture and pack it into the belly cavity of each fish.

6 Cut out 4 double-thickness pieces of greaseproof paper or foil large enough to wrap each fish generously. Grease them with the remaining butter.

7 Wrap each fish in paper or foil, leaving some air space inside the parcel. Twist the top edges of the paper or foil together firmly, and twist the ends to prevent juices escaping.

8 Bake the fish parcels for 20 minutes. Test one to see if it is cooked. Serve them as they are, or with the tops of the parcels turned back and trimmed.

WHOLE STUFFED HADDOCK

Your fish will look dramatic, served upright, as if swimming on the dish. Skewered into an 'S' shape, it cannot fall over. Give it a crusty coat of browned crumbs.

Serve the fish with a sauce-boat of creamy smooth velouté sauce which will add richness to the white fish and herb stuffing.

SERVES 4
1 fresh haddock weighing about 900 g [2 lb]
salt and pepper
1 lemon
100 g [¼ lb] basic stuffing (see recipe)
1 small egg
35 g [1½ oz] dark rye bread
60 ml [4 tablespoons] butter

1 Prepare the breadcrumbs by grating the bread, then brown the crumbs in a warm oven, 160°C [325°F] gas mark 3 for 20 minutes. Make the stuffing as described.

2 Raise the oven heat to 180°C [350°F] gas mark 4 once the breadcrumbs have been removed.

3 Rinse and scale the fish but leave the head and tail on. Clean the belly, rinse and dry it. Season the cavity with a little salt and pepper and a squeeze of lemon juice.

4 Fill the cavity loosely with stuffing, leaving room for the stuffing to swell. Sew up the opening or skewer the sides together with small cocktail sticks.

5 Skewer the fish into an 'S' shape. To do this, bend the fish so that the side of the head almost touches the body. Drive a long skewer through the gills into the middle of the body. Use the same method to skewer the tail to the opposite side of the fish.

6 Set the fish upright on a sheet of greaseproof paper so that the cavity slit is underneath.

7 Beat the egg. Brush it all over the fish. Cover the fish with the browned crumbs and press them on to make a firm coating.

8 Use 15 ml [1 tablespoon] of the butter to grease a shallow ovenproof baking dish which will just hold the fish.

9 Place the fish in the dish, discarding the greaseproof paper. Melt the remaining butter, and sprinkle some of it over the fish. Reserve the rest.

10 Bake the fish for 25-35 minutes. Baste twice during baking with the reserved melted butter.

11 Test whether the fish is done by piercing the flesh with a skewer through the coating.

12 When the fish is tender, raise the oven heat to 230°C [450°F] gas mark 8 for 2-3 minutes, to crisp the coating.

13 Remove the skewers. Serve in the dish or on a warmed serving platter.

ROLLED STUFFED HERRINGS

Serve this attractive yet economical dish hot for a substantial main course. For a summer lunch, chill it and serve it sliced on a bed of lettuce so that its 'pinwheel' circles of stuffing show. Remember to use oil for greasing the dish if serving cold. A salad of golden sweetcorn goes well with either dish.

SERVES 4
4 small herrings, each weighing 225-275 g [½-¾ lb]
salt and pepper
half a lemon
30 ml [2 tablespoons] freshly chopped parsley
200 g [7 oz] roe stuffing
1 medium-sized egg
50 g [2 oz] bread
75 g [3 oz] butter

1 Heat the oven to 190°C [375°F] gas mark 5 and prepare the stuffing.

2 Cut off the fins, heads and tails of the fish, and scale them. Slit open along the length of the belly cavity. Rinse all the bones.

3 Lay the fish flat, cut surface down, and press along the backbone to loosen it. Turn the fish over, and remove all the bones.

4 Season the cut surface lightly with salt and pepper and a squeeze of lemon juice. Place the fish in a dish, cover and put aside.

5 Make the bread into crumbs. Melt 50 g [2 oz] of the butter over low heat and fry the crumbs, stirring constantly, until golden brown.

6 Cover the cut surface of the fish with stuffing and press it down firmly into an even layer.

7 Roll up each fish like a swiss roll, beginning at the tail end. Skewer the ends with wooden cocktail sticks, to fasten them.

8 Beat the egg. Brush the rolls with beaten egg, then coat them with the fried crumbs.

9 Butter a shallow baking dish with the remaining butter. (Use oil if serving cold.) Put in the herring rolls with the cocktail sticks tucked underneath.

10 Bake the rolls for 20-30 minutes, uncovered. Baste occasionally.

11 Remove the cocktail sticks and serve immediately.

12 Alternatively, remove the rolls to a cold dish and allow to become cold. Slice them across, then lay in overlapping lines on a bed of lettuce.

FISH FILLETS AU GRATIN

This makes a lovely dish for a dinner party if you use fillets of plaice or whiting. To make a family dish which is still a great treat, use cod, haddock or coley fillet, but cut the fish into much smaller strips than the above fish. Serve the golden-topped fish garnished with slices of tomato and accompanied by crisp French fried potatoes and garden peas.

SERVES 4
8 thin fish fillets weighing in total about 700 g [1½ lb]
salt and white pepper
half a lemon
pinch of grated or ground nutmeg
50 g [2 oz] butter
100 ml [4 fl oz] white wine
2 shallots
100 g [¼ lb] button mushrooms
10 ml [2 teaspoons] freshly chopped parsley

For the sauce:
25 g [1 oz] butter
20 g [¾ oz] flour
salt and pepper
150 ml [¼ pt] thin cream

For the gratin:
15 g [½ oz] Gruyère cheese
25 g [1 oz] fried breadcrumbs

1 Heat the oven to 180°C [350°F] gas mark 4. Skin the fillets if preferred. Pat them dry and season them lightly with salt, pepper, a squeeze of lemon juice and a pinch of nutmeg.

2 Use 25 g [1 oz] of the butter to grease a shallow baking dish and a piece of foil or greaseproof paper large enough to cover the dish.

3 Fold the fillets in half. Place them in the dish, side by side, with the tail end underneath. Pour the wine and the same quantity of water round them. Cover the dish with the foil or greaseproof paper.

4 Put the dish in the oven and bake the fillets for 10 minutes.

5 Peel and chop the shallots. Melt the remaining butter in the pan. Add the shallots and fry them gently for 2 minutes.

6 Wipe the mushrooms with a damp cloth, trim the stalks and chop the mushrooms. Add them to the pan and fry for 3-4 minutes until just soft. Stir in the parsley.

7 Spread the mixture in the bottom of a warmed serving dish.

8 By now the fish fillets should be cooked. Turn the oven to its lowest temperature—110°C [225°F] gas mark ¼. Remove the dish from the oven. Lift the fillets out of the dish with a perforated spoon and lay them on the shallots and mushrooms. Reserve the liquid in the baking dish.

9 Cover the serving dish loosely with the buttered paper or foil, and put it in the oven while you make the sauce.

10 Melt the butter for the sauce very gently over low heat in a small saucepan. Stir in the flour off the heat. Make a white roux and cook briefly, stirring all the time. Do not let the flour colour.

11 Remove from the heat and stir in the fish cooking liquid gradually. Return to heat and cook, stirring all the time, until the sauce thickens, about 2-3 minutes. Season with a little salt and pepper.

12 Remove from heat and stir in the cream. Return the pan to the heat and cook gently until the sauce re-thickens. Check the seasoning.

13 Grate Gruyère. Mix the crumbs and cheese. Take the serving dish from the oven, remove the covering and pour in the sauce. Sprinkle on the grated cheese and the breadcrumbs evenly to form a gratin over the sauce.

14 Garnish the dish and serve immediately.

In the swim

Cooking fish in liquid can provide some of the finest, most delicious dishes. Poaching is often mismanaged: the fish is boiled rather than poached and most of its flavour thrown down the drain. Given the right cooking liquid for the type of fish, the right quantity and the correct temperature, you will produce fish dishes which are moist and firm with a subtle flavour.

Poaching is the correct way to cook fish in liquid. Poaching on top of the cooker is suitable for large whole fish, both round and flat, for fillets and for smoked fish. Poached fish make ideal meals for children, invalids or slimmers. More than that, fish is poached for many of the most delicious haute cuisine dishes; these are especially good when sauce is made from the poaching liquor—a far cry from soggy, tasteless boiled cod!

Poaching is not the same as boiling. Once the liquid has been brought up to simmering point, the heat must be reduced immediately. The temperature should not exceed 88°C [190°F], which is a very bare simmer. The liquid should quiver around the fish but not bubble.

The only time fish should ever be boiled is when you are making soup or stock. Cheap fish or trimmings are then boiled deliberately, so that all the fish flavour is given up to the liquid.

Poaching does not break up the fish as boiling does. Nor does it make the kitchen smell of fish. It keeps delicate fish flavour where it ought to be—trapped in the fish. Poaching leaves the cooked fish near to its natural state, letting the fish 'speak for itself'.

Truite au bleu is a classic dish and is best served simply with melted butter.

GOLDEN RULES FOR POACHING

The fish must be absolutely fresh. It goes stale quickly once out of water and any hint of staleness will be detectable when the fish is poached because the method shows up the fish's natural flavour. Apart from this, the fresher the fish the sweeter and more delicate its flavour. Moreover, fresh fish keeps its shape better.

The liquid should be chosen to suit the particular fish and should be used at the correct temperature. The chart gives the various types of liquid that can be used and the fish with which each is used.

Use as little liquid as you can for the size and shape of fish you are cooking. Use a pan which holds the fish snugly without unwanted space around it. Only just cover the fish with liquid—do not submerge it deeply. The less liquid you use the more flavourful your fish will be. If you are making sauce from the poaching liquor, this will also have a more concentrated flavour.

Do not overcook your fish. The timing begins from the moment the liquid reaches simmering point. Watch your clock or set your timer; do not risk wasting time and energy and, above all, the fish. Remember that it will go on cooking, if only very slightly, even after you have taken it off the heat. A chart of poaching times is given.

Presentation is particularly important with fish. Even perfectly cooked fish can be spoiled by poor presentation. Always remember to drain poached fish well. Lift small pieces out of the liquid with a perforated fish slice. Transfer larger pieces or whole fish to a board and pat dry before placing on a serving platter.

For most recipes, skin the upper-surface of a whole fish after it is cooked. This is done in much the same way as with a raw fish. Make a nick in the skin just above the tail, hold the skin firmly in one hand and with the other carefully loosen and lift the skin from the flesh with the blunt side of a knife. If it does not come off in one piece, simply scrape the remaining bits and pieces off gently with the knife. There is no need to skin the under-surface of the fish as a rule.

Garnishes should be colourful to overcome the blandness of the white fish flesh.

A fish kettle is a heavy piece of equipment not often seen nowadays.

PREPARING FISH

It is always easier to ask the fishmonger to clean and gut the fish for you but you can, of course, do this yourself if you prefer. Round fish are dealt with on pages 4–5 and flat fish on pages 26–27. Take the fish out of its packaging as soon as you get home, rinse it in cold running water and drain thoroughly. Keep the fish chilled, lightly covered with polythene or foil.

If the fishmonger has cleaned the fish for you, a little seasoning and a squeeze of lemon will improve the flavour and texture. If you are cleaning the fish yourself, this is better done as near cooking time as possible. However, no harm will be done if the preparation is done a few hours in advance. Add lemon juice and seasoning before chilling.

Clean the fish, rinse it, season it and keep covered and chilled until needed. Fillets may be simply wiped with a damp cloth, seasoned with salt, pepper and a squeeze of lemon and kept covered and chilled until needed. Smoked fish needs no preparation—simply keep refrigerated.

EQUIPMENT AND HOW TO USE IT

To poach the fish on top of the cooker you will need a large pan, preferably with some type of rack to keep the fish off the base of the pan, and also some means of getting the fish in and out of the poaching liquor.

Fish kettle. The classic way to poach a large whole fish such as a salmon or a chicken turbot is in a fish kettle. This is a large, deep pan, usually oval in shape with a flat perforated plate which fits inside. It is not elevated as in a steamer but supports the fish just above the base of the pan. Thus the liquid covers the fish (which is then poached) and is not below the level of the fish as it would be in a steamer.

The perforated plate is fitted with two tall handles so that the fish can be lowered in and lifted out easily, without burning your arms on the sides of the pan. When the liquid in the pan is ready for use the fish is laid on the plate and lowered into place. At the end of cooking time it is lifted out again, still on the plate, without risk of it breaking up. Any liquid drains back into the pan through the perforations.

Improvised fish kettles. If you have not got a fish kettle, don't worry. Few people have one these days as it is a

Fish can be poached on top of the cooker or in the oven. Poaching on the top of the cooker is suitable for large whole fish, fillets and smoked fish. Oven poaching, which is better suited to steaks and portions of fish and is also used for fillets, is discussed on page 61.

When poaching on top of the cooker, there is basically one method for large fish and one method for small fish and fillets. Smoked fish are treated in the same way as small fish and fillets, or they can be poached without additional heat by the 'jug' method.

The important difference between the method for large fish and the method for small fish is the temperature of the liquid at the point at which the fish is immersed.

Large fish

For large whole fish or a large portion of a whole fish the liquid must be cool to start with. If you were to immerse a large whole fish in near-boiling water, this would cause the skin to shrink and burst. The liquid is brought slowly to just below boiling point (simmering point) and this slow treatment allows the heat to penetrate right through the fish. If hot liquid were used, the outer part of the fish would cook too quickly while the inside remained cold and raw.

To poach the fish place it on the trivet, rack, oiled greaseproof paper or foil then pour in the liquid to barely cover the fish. It is important that the fish should be a good fit for the pan or an unnecessarily large amount of liquid will be needed. Cover the pan and bring slowly to simmering point. When the first bubble appears, reduce the heat to just below the simmering point. The liquid should quiver around the fish with not a bubble in sight. Poach for the time appropriate for the weight of the fish. Poaching times are given in the chart.

Small fish, fillets and smoked fish

If you are poaching small fish or pieces of fish it is not necessary to start with cool liquid. The liquid should be near simmering as heat is needed to seal the open surface of fillets. This prevents the flavour dispersing into the liquid. The gentle warming that is required for large fish is also unnecessary.

large piece of equipment for large fish, and large numbers. Improvisation is easy and successful. The bonus of the fish kettle is the supporting perforated plate. There are two quick and simple methods for improvising this plate, but you will need a pan large enough to hold the fish. Although it must be large it must not be unnecessarily so.

For the fish pan you can use a preserving pan, a solid roasting tin, casserole dish or any flameproof pan deep enough and long enough to hold the fish and the liquid. A lid can be made from foil or greaseproof paper, as it does not have to be airtight.

You also need something on which to lie the fish to make handling easier and, if possible, to raise it off the bottom of the pan. A small roasting trivet, cake rack or the grid from the grill pan is ideal if it will fit the chosen pan.

If you have none of these, cut a double thickness of foil large enough for the fish to lie on, grease it lightly with very little oil, and place the fish on it. Alternatively, wrap the fish in lightly oiled greaseproof paper and secure with string.

You will also need some help with lifting the fish in and out of the pan, to prevent it from breaking up. Cut a piece of muslin large enough to wrap round the fish and its support, including the rack or grid if either is being used, long enough for the ends to hang over the sides of the pan. Wrapping the fish in this way also helps it to keep its shape. If you have not got any muslin, a trivet, cake rack or grid can be lifted out fairly easily without it. A fish lying on foil or wrapped in greaseproof paper will have to be raised with the aid of fish slices or slings made of foil.

To make the slings of foil, cut two double-thickness pieces of foil long enough to go under the width of the fish and hang over the sides of the pan. Put one piece under the fish towards the head and the other towards the tail. When the fish is cooked, draw the ends of each sling together, take the pieces at the head in one hand and the pieces at the tail in the other (or however suits you) and lift the fish out on to a board.

Poaching small fish and fillets

Small fish and fillets, being light in weight, do not need a supporting base. The fish can be poached in a shallow pan covered with a lid, foil or greaseproof paper, or a flat baking tray. The fish is easily removed from the pan with the aid of a perforated fish slice.

43

Ingredients	Making the liquid	Using the liquid
BRINE 100 g [¼ lb] salt 1 bay leaf (optional)	Add the salt to 1.7 L [3 pt] water to make a strong brine. Use seawater if you can with less salt. A bay leaf floating on top is optional.	The brine should be cool. Poach fresh salmon for time given in recipe.
SIMPLE COURT-BOUILLON 8 black peppercorns 1 medium-sized onion 30 ml [2 tablespoons] white wine vinegar salt	Crush peppercorns coarsely. Peel and slice onion. Mix all ingredients with 1.2 L [2 pt] water, heat to simmering point and simmer, uncovered, for 30 minutes. Allow to cool and check seasoning before use.	Start with cool liquid for large fish, near simmering for small. Poach fish for time given in recipe. Discard liquid after use.
SIMPLE WHITE COURT-BOUILLON 550 ml [1 pt] milk 1 lemon slice salt and pepper	Mix all ingredients with 550 ml [1 pt] water.	Start with cool liquid for large fish or pieces. Heat and use at boiling point for jugging. Discard lemon and use liquid for sauce.
GENERAL-PURPOSE COURT-BOUILLON 10 black peppercorns 3 cloves bouquet garni 550 ml [1 pt] dry white wine or dry cider 1 large carrot 1 large mild onion 2 small leeks 7.5 ml [1½ teaspoons] pickling spice	Crush peppercorns coarsely. Tie herbs and spices in muslin. Peel and slice leeks. Mix all ingredients with 550 ml [1 pt] water. Heat to simmering point and simmer, uncovered, for 30 minutes. Allow to cool and check seasoning before use.	Start with cool liquid. Poach fish for time given in recipe. Strain liquid after use and use as basis for fish soups or mild sauces.
REDUCED COURT-BOUILLON Ingredients as for general-purpose court-bouillon.	Prepare and mix as above. Bring to boil and boil rapidly, uncovered, to reduce by half.	Start with near simmering liquid. (Put shellfish in boiling liquid.) Poach fish for time given in recipe. Strain liquid after use and use for sauces.
FISH FUMET (CONCENTRATED FISH STOCK) 900 g–1.4 kg [2–3 lb] fish bones, trimmings and heads, including those of turbot and sole if possible 700 g [1½ lb] cheap white fish 1 large onion 1 medium-sized carrot 1 leek 5 cm [2"] celery stick 8 black peppercorns 10 ml [2 teaspoons] white wine vinegar 200 ml [7 fl oz] dry white wine	Peel and slice onion and carrot. Clean and slice white part of leek, chop celery. Put all ingredients in a large pan with enough water to cover. Bring to the boil and skim. Lower heat and simmer, uncovered, for 20–30 minutes. Strain at once through muslin-lined sieve. Keep hot for small fish and fillets, cool for poaching large fish.	Use as for reduced court bouillon above.

Suitable fish

Fat, silvery early-season salmon, grilse, shellfish.

Mature, and thinner, reddish salmon, whole oily fish such as trout and mackerel.

Smoked white fish (haddock, cod), kippers, turbot, brill and halibut.

Any large whole fish or portions of fish.

Any small fish, fillets or shellfish.

Any fish recipe which needs fish fumet.

POACHING TIMES FOR FISH

Small thin fillets /portions shellfish	3–5 minutes
Smoked fish (jugged)	5–10 minutes
Medium /thick fillets	6–10 minutes
Steaks /cutlets /portions, according to thickness	8–15 minutes
Small whole fish (eg sole, whiting, plaice)	8–15 minutes
Whole fish or piece of fish, 700 g [1½ lb] to 900 g [2 lb]	8–15 minutes
Whole fish, 900 g [2 lb] to 1.8 kg [4 lb]	15–18 minutes
Whole fish, 2 kg [4½ lb] to 2.7 kg [6 lb]	20–30 minutes
Larger fish, according to thickness, per 450 g [1 lb]	5–10 minutes

Place the fillets and small fish in the pan. Heat the liquid in a separate pan to near simmering. Pour this round and over the fish until it is just covered. The liquid is then brought to just below simmering point. At the appearance of the first bubble in the liquid, reduce the heat immediately to maintain a very gentle simmer. There should not be any bubbles on the surface of the liquid, just a gentle quivering.

Small flat fish may have a tendency to curl when placed in hot water and cooked fairly quickly. A good tip is to slit the fish down the backbone on the dark skinned side, and carefully snip the backbone in two places. To snip the backbone simply raise it in two places with the point of a pair of scissors, slip one blade underneath and snip through. Two cuts should be sufficient to hold the fish flat while it is cooking. Smooth the flesh back once the backbone has been cut.

POACHING TIMES

Poaching times may vary according to whether the fish has fine or coarse flesh, whether it is in a solid piece, and whether, if it is filleted, it is cooked flat or rolled. Fish is cooked when the flesh is opaque all through or when a little creamy curd appears between the scales and the flesh parts easily from the bone when the point of a skewer is inserted.

NO-COOK POACHING METHODS

There are two no-cook ways of poaching fish—one is ideal for smoked fish, and the other for a large whole fish to be served cold.

The 'jug' method

Kippers, bloaters and other small whole smoked fish can be poached without being cooked at all and can be served hot or cold.

Choose a heatproof jug into which you can lower the fish without folding or bending it. It should be deep enough to hold the whole fish except the inedible tip of the tail.

Lower the fish into the jug, head first, and pour the liquid, which should be boiling, over it. Fill the jug completely. Leave it to stand for 5–10 minutes; do not leave it any longer or the fish will go soggy. Pull the fish out gently by its tail, lay it on kitchen paper and pat dry.

Step-by-step to poaching a large fish

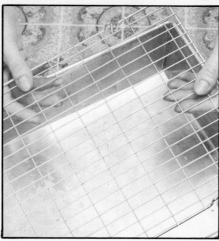

1 Have cooled court-bouillon ready. Choose a pan and equipment for lifting and supporting the fish.

2 Cut two long, double-thickness pieces of foil. Fold to make two long slings. Place under the rack.

5 Time cooking period from point of simmering. Poach for the time specified in chart. Test fish.

6 Lift the fish and rack out with the foil slings allowing the liquid to drain back into the pan.

Step-by-step to 'jugging'

1 Choose a tall heatproof jug deep enough to hold the whole fish except the inedible tail tip.

2 Bring a simple white court-bouillon to the boil. Lower the fish, head first, into the jug.

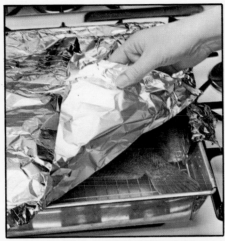

3 Lower the prepared fish into the pan. Pour in the court-bouillon to barely cover. Cover with lid.

4 Place over low heat. Bring just to simmering point. Reduce heat immediately and poach gently.

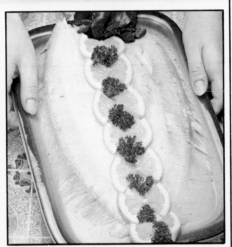

7 Lay fish on a board, dark skin up. Skin carefully with the aid of a knife and keep fish hot.

8 Make sauce from court-bouillon. Place fish on serving plate and garnish well. Serve with sauce.

3 Pour in the boiling liquid. Leave the fish to stand for 5–10 minutes, no longer.

4 Withdraw the fish gently by the tip of the tail, lay it flat on kitchen paper and pat dry.

If you wish to poach fillets of smoked fish in this manner or do not possess a tall heatproof jug, use a saucepan or other dish in which the fish can lie flat. Pour on the boiling liquid, cover with a lid or foil, and leave for 5–10 minutes. Remove the fish with a perforated fish slice, drain and pat dry. It is necessary to cover the dish or pan as the area of evaporation is far greater than that of the tall jug.

The jug method is a particularly good way of handling kippers or bloaters which you suspect may be very salty. The jugging will make them moist, less oily and less salty.

Cold start for serving cold

This method keeps the fish beautifully moist which is very important when the fish is to be served cold.

Place the whole fish in its cooking container on its supporting base. Pour in the cool liquid to barely cover the fish. Bring the liquid gently to the boil and let it bubble gently for 2–3 minutes, no longer. Remove the pan from the heat and let the fish cool in the liquid.

The beauty of this method is that the process is absolutely simple as there is no cooking time to calculate. It does not matter what size the fish is. The quantity of liquid used and the time it takes to reach the boil and then to cool down again and cool the fish will ensure that a fish of any size will be cooked right through. Wait until the fish is completely cold before removing it from the liquid.

If you are serving fillets this method cannot be used. Treat the fish as though you were serving it hot. When cooked, remove from the pan, drain thoroughly and place on the serving platter. Allow to become cool, cover and keep chilled.

Handy hints

Fish is always improved by the inclusion of wine in the cooking liquid. If you have no wine for the court-bouillons in the chart, you can use instead:
- dry cider or a mixture of cider and water
- $\frac{2}{3}$ quantity of fish stock with $\frac{1}{3}$ quantity of white wine vinegar with a pinch of sugar
- dry vermouth and water mixed half and half.

SOLE VERONIQUE

This classic dish was named after the first-born child of one of the chefs; she was born the day the dish was created. Seedless white grapes are added to the fish in its creamy sauce. You will need a quantity of béchamel sauce for this recipe and this can be prepared in advance or while the fish fumet is simmering. Have this ready in a small saucepan. Make the fish fumet as described in the chart on poaching liquids.

SERVES 4

8 fillets of sole weighing in total about 700 g [1½ lb]
salt and white pepper
550 ml [1 pt] fish fumet
100 g [¼ lb] seedless white grapes
150 ml [¼ pt] béchamel sauce
2 medium-sized eggs
60 ml [4 tablespoons] thick cream
30 ml [2 tablespoons] softened butter

1 Season the fillets with salt and pepper and lay them flat in a shallow flameproof dish. Pour over sufficient fumet to cover.

2 Bring the pan to simmering point and adjust heat immediately to maintain a bare simmer. Poach the fillets for 6–8 minutes depending on thickness.

3 Lift the fillets out of the dish with a perforated fish slice. Reserve the fumet in the dish. Drain the fillets well and lay on a serving dish. Keep warm.

4 Pick the stems off the grapes and drop them into near boiling water to heat through. Remove them from the water after a few moments using a perforated spoon. Drain well and arrange around the fish.

5 Taste the fish fumet remaining in the flameproof dish. Boil for a few minutes to reduce if a stronger flavour is needed. Measure off 250 ml [½ pt] fumet and strain into the pan holding the béchamel sauce; stir in while pouring.

6 Separate the eggs and reserve the whites for another dish. Cream together the yolks and 30 ml [2 tablespoons] cream.

7 Add 30 ml [2 tablespoons] of warm sauce mixture to the cream and yolks, blend thoroughly and then stir into the sauce.

8 Heat the sauce slowly without boiling, stirring continuously, until it thickens. Place the pan in a baking tin containing hot water to keep warm.

9 Heat the grill to hot. Whip the remaining cream until thick but not stiff. Stir the butter into the sauce and then add the whipped cream.

10 Pour the sauce over the fish and the grapes. Place under grill for about a minute to brown lightly, and serve immediately.

TWO TURBOT MEALS IN ONE

◨◨◨ *Justify the expense of this large prime fish by making two distinctive meals with it, one served hot and the other cold. The hot dish is served with a bowl of freshly grated horseradish and a sauce-boat of melted butter, and the chilled turbot is covered with a herb-flavoured vinaigrette dressing.*

Serve the hot dish for dinner one evening and the turbot vinaigrette for a light lunch with crusty brown bread and butter the next day. The second dish has a completely different flavour from the hot dish served the night before.

SERVES 4 (TWICE)
**1.8 kg [4 lb] chicken turbot
about 1.7 L [3 pt] general-
     purpose court-bouillon**

Cold turbot with vinaigrette dressing is the second meal from one fish. A lemon and watercress garnish adds a touch of colour.

**For the hot garnish:
1 large egg
20 ml [1¼ tablespoons] butter
15 ml [1 tablespoon] parsley
1 lemon**

**For the cold garnish:
150 ml [¼ pt] vinaigrette
     dressing
22.5 ml [1½ tablespoons] mixed
     fresh parsley, tarragon and
     chives
1 egg
6 capers
5 walnuts**

1 Gut the fish if this has not already been done, wipe with a damp cloth and place, dark side uppermost, in a genuine or improvised fish kettle. Make a muslin or 2 foil slings and put slings under the fish to aid removal.

2 Pour in enough general-purpose court-bouillon just to cover the fish.

3 Bring the liquid to simmering point slowly, and adjust heat to maintain a bare simmer. Poach the fish for 15–18 minutes or until tender.

4 Hard boil both the eggs (one for the hot dish, one for the cold). Plunge them into cold water, shell and leave in cold water until needed.

5 Remove the fish from the heat. Lift the fish out of the liquid on to a board. Pat the fish dry.

6 Skin the upper dark-skinned surface of the fish. Trim the fins and cut down along the backbone. Remove the upper two fillets from the fish, loosening and lifting each fillet from the bone. This will leave the head and tail intact with the backbone and the two fillets underneath. The upper, thicker fillets are served hot. The rest of the fish should be allowed to become cool, covered loosely with foil and chilled.

7 Place the two fillets close together on a serving platter to look like a fish. Melt 20 ml [1½ tablespoons] butter over a low heat and brush most of it over the turbot. Use the rest to butter a piece of grease-proof paper, cover the turbot and keep warm.

8 Chop one hard-boiled egg evenly, and chop the parsley finely.

9 Slice the lemon thinly to get enough slices to cover the length of the turbot.

10 Lay the slices of lemon down the centre of the turbot fillets, to hide the join. Scatter over the chopped egg and parsley and serve immediately.

11 To serve the turbot vinaigrette lay the fish in a shallow serving dish with the backbone uppermost. Remove the backbone by snipping through at the head and tail, loosening with a knife, and lifting out. Leave the head and tail in place if you wish, or remove.

12 Finely chop the mixed fresh herbs and mix into the vinaigrette. Chop the remaining hard-boiled egg, the capers and the nuts and stir into the dressing. Check the seasoning and pour over the fish.

13 Cover the dish lightly and chill the fish for at least 4 hours with its dressing.

SKATE WITH BLACK BUTTER

Once despised, we now appreciate the lovely flavour of this easily-digested, rosy-white fish. It has a soft bone, unlike the normal spiky fish bones, from which the flesh parts willingly, making the eating easier and all the more enjoyable. The pieces of skate which we eat are nearly always from the wing, and the whole kite-shaped creature is a rare sight.

Black butter (beurre noir) is traditional with wing of skate and is quick and simple to make. In a basic recipe the proportion of vinegar is less, but the amount of vinegar in this recipe has been increased for extra zest.

SERVES 4
1 kg [2¼ lb] wing of skate
**1 L [1¾ pt] simple
  court-bouillon**

For the beurre noir:
75 g [3 oz] unsalted butter
15 ml [1 tablespon] capers
**15 ml [1 tablespoon] white
  wine vinegar**

1 Cut the skate into serving portions; the bone is easy to cut through although it looks tough.

2 Place the skate portions in one layer in a shallow flameproof pan or baking tin, or a deep skillet.

3 Pour the cool court-bouillon over the skate, just covering it. Bring slowly to simmering point, then adjust the heat to maintain a bare simmer. Cover and poach for 8–15 minutes, until the skate is tender.

5 Transfer the skate from the pan to a board. Scrape off any skin with the blunt side of a knife. Place the fish on a warmed serving dish, and keep warm while making the beurre noir.

6 Melt the butter in a heavy-based pan over low heat and cook very gently until it turns dark golden brown. This will take about 1 minute.

7 Meanwhile chop the capers. Add the vinegar and capers to the butter, stir once and remove from heat.

8 Pour the black butter over the skate and serve immediately.

FILETS DE MERLAN A LA DIEPPOISE

This is a simple yet good dish from a French port renowned as a fishing centre. It is worth taking time over although its ingredients seem quite ordinary. The liquid from the mussels is used in place of a court-bouillon. You can use canned mussels but these must be in brine, not in vinegar. You will need a 150 g [5 oz] can. Fresh mussels must be cleaned carefully. This process is described in detail on pages 124–25 in the Star Recipe for moules à la marinière.

SERVES 4
1.15 L [2 pt] fresh mussels
**8 whiting fillets weighing, in
  total, about 700 g [1½ lb]**
salt and pepper
**175 g [6 oz] button
  mushrooms**
half a lemon
75 g [3 oz] butter
250 ml [½ pt] dry white wine
**30 ml [2 tablespoons] plain
  flour**

1 Put cleaned fresh mussels in a large shallow pan. Cover and place over gentle heat. Shake the pan gently until the mussels open. Throw out any which remain shut.

2 Drain all the liquor from the fresh mussels into a bowl. Remove fresh mussels from shells and reserve the flesh. Discard the shells.

3 If using canned mussels, drain off the brine and dilute with water to give a lightly salted flavour.

4 Season the whiting fillets with salt and pepper, and lay them flat in a flameproof pan, side by side.

50

5 Wipe the mushrooms with a damp cloth and trim the stalks. Squeeze the juice from the lemon and sprinkle the mushrooms with it. Melt a third of the butter. Fry the mushrooms gently until just soft. Remove the mushrooms and reserve with the mussels.

6 Pour the butter and mushroom juice over the whiting. Add the wine and sufficient mussel liquor or diluted brine to just cover the fish.

7 Bring the liquor to simmering point and adjust the heat immediately to maintain a bare simmer. Poach the fish for 6–10 minutes. Be careful not to overcook.

8 Lift the whiting with a perforated fish slice on to a warmed serving dish. Surround with the reserved mussels and fried mushrooms and keep warm. Reserve the poaching liquid in the dish.

9 Heat the grill to hot. Boil the poaching liquid for 3–4 minutes to reduce it a little.

10 Meanwhile, cream together the remaining butter and the flour to make a smooth paste (beurre manié).

11 Over low heat, stir the buerre manié into the liquid in small spoonfuls, and stir until melted. Simmer gently until the sauce thickens, stirring continuously.

12 Pour the sauce over the fish. Place under the hot grill for a minute or two, to brown the top. Serve at once.

Three poached fish dishes with very different flavours: whiting with mussels and mushrooms, buttery skate with capers and creamy sole Véronique with grapes.

TRUITE AU BLEU

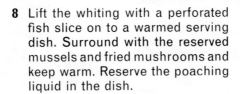
Cooking trout in this way makes the natural slime on their skins turn a dreamy slate blue. The fish should be live but if you have no fisherman in the family to produce live trout, you can use fresh trout from the fishmonger. Cooked, these will be greyish rather than blue. The important thing is not to wash the natural sheen from the skin. Do not mask the fish or hide its flavour with a thick sauce. Rather, serve the fish just with melted clarified butter and its traditional garnish of lemon quarters and chopped parsley. To make clarified butter, melt and strain through a muslin-lined sieve.

SERVES 4
4 medium-sized live or fresh trout
2.3 L [4 pt] simple court-bouillon
2 lemons
45 ml [3 tablespoons] freshly chopped parsley
175 g [6 oz] clarified butter

1 Kill the trout with a sharp blow on the back of the head. Gut the fish but handle them as little as possible. Do not cut off the fins, scrape or rinse.

2 Place the fish in a large flameproof dish or saucepan. Pour over just enough very hot court-bouillon to cover them. Bring to simmering point and adjust heat immediately to maintain a bare simmer. Poach 8–15 minutes, depending on size. Test the fish with a thin skewer after 8 minutes and continue cooking if necessary.

3 Meanwhile, quarter the lemons and chop the parsley.

4 Put the clarified butter in a small pan to melt over a low heat.

5 When the trout is cooked, remove the pan from the heat, and discard the court-bouillon. Slide the fish, or lift out gently, on to a warmed serving platter. Tilt the platter to drain off any remaining court-bouillon. Mop up with soft kitchen paper around the fish.

6 Sprinkle the parsley over the fish and garnish with lemon wedges. Pour the melted butter into a heated sauce-boat and serve immediately.

Fisherman's fare

Enjoy a real fisherman's meal with fresh fish, locally grown vegetables and herbs and some well-flavoured liquid. Every variety of fish can be used, either by itself or mixed with other fish—and nearly all the meals can be prepared in under an hour. Many fish stews, created by villagers from ingredients immediately to hand, have become part of classical French cuisine.

Stews and casseroles made with fish fresh from the sea are real fishermen's meals. All the unusual fish collected in a fisherman's nets and not sold on the quayside went into his family's cooking pot. In times gone by this was literally one big iron pot on the open fire, and the fisherman's wife put everything into it. The assorted fish with locally grown vegetables and herbs made a simmering rich broth which was ladled out and the solid food made a fragrant main-course dish.

These one-pot meals are still served everywhere. From north to south, in Europe and America, every coastal community makes its own version. The ingredients and flavour-ings vary to some extent in differing climates, but the method does not. The reason for their continuing popularity, since we do not now have to cook in one pot, is that they offer real value; the extra ingredients used are nearly always cheap. Exotic and extravagant vegetables and fruit are not necessary, nor are rich dairy products.

STEW OR CASSEROLE?

A fish stew and a fish casserole use much the same ingredients, although technically a stew should be cooked on the top of the stove and a casserole in the oven. As when made with meat, these words are used interchangeably nowadays. The main difference, when fish is used, is the quantity of liquid.

A fish stew is really a nourishing fish soup flavoured by the fish and vegetables which are cooked in it. The stew can be served as it is or can be served as two courses: the strained broth, followed by the fish and vegetables as a main course. The pot contains a substantial amount of liquid.

A casserole contains less liquid than a stew, sometimes just enough to make a sauce, and cannot be served as two courses. The fish is not cut up as it is in a stew and the resulting dish is more similar to a baked dish than to a stew.

PRINCIPLES OF STEWING FISH

When making a fish soup, the fish is boiled so that it gives up all its goodness and flavour to the liquid. The fleshy remnants are then strained out and only the liquid is served.

The dishes described in this course are different: they are a combination of a soup and a stew. The fish is cooked so that it keeps its nourishment and juices, and vegetables and herbs are added to flavour both the fish and the liquid. If the liquid is already a well-flavoured fish stock prepared from fish trimmings so much the better.

The method

The cooking method is simple in theory and practice. The vegetables that are to be included in the dish are fried briefly in hot fat or oil, in the stew pan. The cooking liquid and herbs are added and the pan is heated gently until the contents are boiling. The fish, usually cut up into chunks, is put straight into the boiling liquid so that the heat stiffens the outer flesh at once, sealing in the juices. The heat under the pan is lowered and the fish is cooked in simmering liquid for a short time: barely long enough for it to cook through. It is preferable, in fact, to slightly undercook the fish as it will continue to cook slightly in its own heat after it has been strained from the liquid.

The important fact is that the liquid must always be hot when it comes into contact with the fish. If it is added to the pan after the fish, it should be heated to boiling point first. In some recipes, where extra oil would be unpleasant, the vegetables are not fried first but are simply cooked in the hot liquid with the fish.

PRINCIPLES OF CASSEROLING FISH

The ingredients of a casserole are virtually identical to a stew except that the quantity of liquid is considerably smaller. It is usually a spicy sauce and not just plain stock. The principles are the same as stewing, in that the fish is sealed to retain its goodness and juices, and vegetables are added to increase the flavour, but the method is different.

The method

The fish is sealed, not in hot liquid but by the acid ingredient, such as lemon juice, wine or soured cream that is included in the liquid. First, as in stewing, the vegetables are put in the bottom of the casserole dish. They are sometimes fried but in other recipes are simply cooked with the fish. The fish goes in next, not cut into chunks, followed by the sauce, or the sauce followed by the fish. The sauce can be added hot or cold as it is the acid that seals the fish. The oven temperature is sufficient to bring the pot to the required temperature and to maintain this temperature throughout cooking. The liquid should be actually simmering, as in stewing. The fish is served from the casserole dish with the sauce spooned over it.

INGREDIENTS

A fisherman's wife would choose whether she would make a casserole or a stew by the types of fish that were available. This is a sensible rule to follow. If you have firm-fleshed white fish which can be cut easily into chunks, then make a stew. If you have small whole fish, thin fillets or soft fish which may disintegrate in a large quantity of liquid, it is wiser to make a casserole.

Whichever dish you are cooking, the fish must be absolutely fresh. If you cannot get a particular fish that your recipe includes, substitute another of the same type—as the fisherman's wife would. Buying mixed fish for both stewing and casseroling gives you the opportunity to try out one or two of the more unusual fish on display. They are often cheap, not because they are inferior, but because people find them strange. Don't be put off by their appearance. Some, for instance, have odd spiky heads but these can be used to make fish stock and will then be thrown away; only the flesh actually appears on the table.

You can use sea or freshwater fish, although not together. You can, and should, use a proportion of firm oily fish such as eel with your white fish, when you can get it.

You can use fresh or frozen fish and buy it whole, in steaks or fillets and treat it as necessary for your cooking method, when you get home. Cook fresh fish the day you buy it.

Fish for stewing

There is a huge choice of fish that can be used for stewing. The fish needs to be firm because the large quantity of liquid bubbling around the chunks would break them up if they were soft. Choose from the following: brill, carp, char, cod, coley, crayfish (rock lobster), grayling, grey mullet, gurnard, haddock, hake, halibut, John Dory, lobster, monkfish, mussels, oysters, pike, pollock, prawns, red mullet, river bass, rock salmon, scallops, sea bream, squid, tench, turbot, weever.

Shellfish, which are discussed in detail on pages 87–95 are absolutely ideal for use in stews as they can

be popped into the hot liquid for the few minutes they take to cook.

Fish for casseroling

Casseroling disturbs the fish very little and enables you to select the softer fish and those that are often sold in thin fillets, such as plaice. The fish lie on a bed of vegetables and can be cooked in steaks or fillets. Casseroling is suitable for coarser flavoured fish which stands up well to the aromatic, pungent flavours used in Spanish, Italian and southern French dishes. Several of the fish suitable for casseroling are firm enough for stewing and appear in both lists. Choose from: carp, cod, dab, flounder, haddock, hake, hali-but, herring, John Dory, mackerel, pike, plaice, red mullet, salmon, salmon trout, sole, tunny, turbot and whiting.

The liquid for stewing

The basic liquid for a fish stew can be just water, or water and milk, but any stew is infinitely better made with stock and a fish stew with fish stock. Use the heads, trimmings, skin and bones of the fish to make a stock, before making the stew itself. If you buy the fish already prepared as steaks or fillets, always ask for some fish heads and bones at the same time. If you buy frozen fish you will either have to buy extra and use some for making the stock, which is rather extravagant, or make do without fish stock.

If you do make your own fish stock, remember it must be used, or frozen, within 24 hours. If frozen, it will keep for up to one month.

The liquid for casseroling

The liquid in a casserole is more likely to be a sauce than plain stock; it gives a richer flavour than stock. The other flavouring liquid which you will find in a number of casseroles from the European continent is wine or another liquor. Both red and white wine can be used despite the tendency to associate white wine with fish and red wine with meat.

Vegetable and flavourings

The liquid provides some of the flavouring for your stew or casserole but other ingredients are always added. Freshly chopped herbs are nearly always included, varying according to where the dish originates from: a Swedish recipe will often include dill, a Spanish one, garlic.

Two flavourings, however, occur in practically every fish stew or casserole. These are onions and parsley which are used frequently, no matter where the recipe comes from.

Other vegetables are often added to the onions and can be cooked in chunks to be served with the fish, or sieved after cooking in order to thicken the liquid or sauce. Tomatoes, potatoes and peppers are often included.

Various other ingredients are used for thickening and bulk in the stews originating from southern Europe and bread, often toasted, appears in recipes from France and Spain.

SOME FAMOUS FISH STEWS

Bouillabaisse is a famous saffron-flavoured fish stew from the Mediterranean coast of France. A true bouillabaisse cannot be made in areas where the scorpion-fish (or rascasse as the French call it) is unobtainable, since this is considered an essential ingredient to the dish.

Bouride, a stew from Provence, is very strongly flavoured with garlic. The soup and the fish are served separately.

Cotriade is a fish stew from Brittany which can be made in many areas because the varieties of fish that the Bretons use are widely available elsewhere. The other main ingredient is potatoes and the Americans have adopted this dish and called it a chowder. Newfoundland and New England are areas associated with chowder.

Matelote is the name given to a stew in which the fish is cooked in wine. Strictly speaking freshwater fish should be used but the dish varies according to the region from which it comes. In the dairy districts of Normandy, for instance, sea fish are used and the stew is thickened with eggs and cream, and cider made from the apples grown locally is included.

Meurette is a matelote from Burgundy (matelote a la bourguignonne) which uses red wine.

PORTUGUESE FISH SOUP

With its hard-boiled eggs, shellfish and a garnish of almonds, this is a handsome dish. It's a quick one too, for you can boil the eggs ahead of time and use frozen prawns.

SERVES 4
225 g [½ lb] fresh, skinned haddock fillet
1 medium-sized onion, finely chopped
30 ml [2 tablespoons] olive oil
1 L [1¾ pts] fish stock
100 g [¼ lb] frozen prawns
30 ml [2 tablespoons] freshly chopped parsley
salt and pepper
2.5 ml [½ teaspoon] dried oregano or tarragon
4 thick slices of bread
2 hard-boiled eggs
10 ml [2 teaspoons] butter
30 ml [2 tablespoons] flaked almonds

1 Put the onion and oil in a saucepan big enough to take all the ingredients. Cut haddock into pieces about 5 cm [2"] in size. Put the fish on the onion.

2 Pour the prepared fish stock into the pan. Add the prawns and parsley. Season well with salt and pepper. Add the herbs.

3 Bring the stock up to simmering point. Skim well. Simmer for 10 minutes, uncovered.

4 While the pan is simmering, toast the bread lightly on both sides. Chop the hard-boiled eggs. Heat the butter in a small pan over low heat and fry almonds until golden.

5 Put the toast into 4 warmed soup bowls. Put a quarter of the chopped egg on each toast slice. Ladle the soup over the toast.

6 Sprinkle the almonds over each bowl and serve at once.

MACKEREL CASSEROLE

Straight from Scandinavia, this quick, simple casserole dish is one of the few using oily fish. It is all the more welcome, since mackerel is so cheap and so good! In this recipe, the lemon juice and acid cream seal the fish as firmly as boiling liquid would.

SERVES 4
2 mackerel, each weighing about 450–700 g [1–1½ lb]
40 g [1½ oz] butter
salt
2 leeks
225 g [½ lb] canned tomatoes
15 ml [1 tablespoon] dill seeds
2.5 ml [½ teaspoon] paprika
juice of half a lemon
150 ml [¼ pt] soured cream

1 Wash and fillet the mackerel and skin if preferred. Heat the oven to 180°C [350°F] gas mark 4.

2 Use 15 g [½ oz] butter to grease the inside of a casserole which will just hold the fillets in one layer and lay the fish in it.

3 Wash the leeks and slice the white part finely. Melt the remaining butter in a frying-pan and sauté the leeks until soft. Add the tomatoes, dill seeds and paprika, mix together and transfer to the casserole.

4 Sprinkle in the lemon juice and pour the sour cream over the top.

5 Cover the dish. Put into the oven and cook for 20 minutes. Serve hot from the dish.

Warming and filling Portuguese fish soup.

SPANISH FISH SUPPER

This is a splendid one-pot family meal for when you are too busy to cook your fish the day you buy it—the marinade will preserve the fish overnight. Any white fish fillet or steaks, such as coley, cod, bass, hake or haddock may be used.

SERVES 4
1 kg [2¼ lb] white fish
4 medium-sized onions
3 garlic cloves
2 parsley sprigs
1 bay leaf
15 ml [1 tablespoon] white
   wine vinegar
75 ml [3 fl oz] olive oil
salt and pepper
50 g [2 oz] plain flour
8 thick slices French bread
15 ml [1 tablespoon] chopped
   chives

1 Skin the fish and remove any bones (keep them for making fish stock). Cut the fish into big pieces, 7.5–10 cm [3–4"] in size.

2 Peel and chop the onions and garlic and chop the parsley coarsely, including the stalks.

3 Put these ingredients into a deep non-corrodible container. Add the bay leaf, vinegar and oil. Season well with salt and pepper.

4 Put in the fish, and turn it over gently to coat thoroughly. Leave it for at least several hours or overnight.

5 In a large saucepan, bring 1.5 L [2½ pt] water to the boil. Add the fish and simmer for one minute. Add all the marinade, including the vegetables and flavourings. Season with salt and pepper.

6 Bring back to the boil. Cover the pan. Lower the heat and simmer for 15 minutes.

7 Mix the flour with 30 ml [2 tablespoons] cold water to make a smooth cream. Add a little of the hot soup and then stir it into the pan of soup. Simmer for another 5 minutes, stirring.

8 Toast the bread very lightly on both sides. Put 2 slices of toast in each of 4 heated individual soup bowls. Gently strain the fish soup, so as not break up the fish, over the bread in the bowls. Place the strained fish in a warmed, shallow dish. Sprinkle it with the chives.

9 Serve a bowl of soup to each person. Hand round the fish and onion mixture separately, so that each person can put some into his soup.

STEWED EELS, 1880

Not all fish stew recipes are imported! This one comes from England's Mrs Beeton. Eels are rich in nourishment and well worth making into a family meal. The stock may be made with a cube.

SERVES 4
1 kg [2¼ lb] eels or 4 conger
   eel steaks weighing about
   225 g [½ lb] each
salt and pepper
2 large onions
4 cloves
1 strip lemon zest
575 ml [1 pt] chicken stock
75 ml [3 fl oz] port or Madeira
75 ml [3 fl oz] thick cream
30 ml [2 tablespoons] flour
cayenne pepper
a few drops of lemon juice

1 If you have bought whole eels, wash and skin them and remove their heads. Cut them into pieces 7.5 cm [3"] long.

2 Lay the pieces of eel or the conger steaks in a stewpan which will just hold them in one layer. Season them with salt and pepper.

3 Peel the onions and stick the cloves into them. Place the onions on the fish. Add the strip of lemon rind.

4 Mix together the stock and the port or Madeira. Bring to the boil in a small saucepan. Pour the liquid over the fish. Bring the pan up to the boil over medium heat.

5 Reduce the heat so that the liquid just simmers. Cover the pan. Simmer for 30 minutes or until the fish is tender.

6 Discard the onions. Take out the pieces of eel or conger with a slotted spoon; drain them over the pan. Put them in a heated shallow serving dish. Keep them warm under buttered paper.

7 In a small bowl, mix the cream and flour. Add a little of the hot liquid from the pan. Blend thoroughly, leaving no lumps.

8 Off the heat, stir this mixture into the sauce in the pan. Replace the pan over moderate heat, and stir until the mixture thickens. Reduce the heat and allow the flour to cook for a few minutes.

9 Stir a few grains of cayenne pepper and a few drops of lemon juice into the sauce. Check the seasoning.

10 Strain the sauce over the fish and serve at once.

Matelote Normande is a particularly tasty fish stew. It is a rich and nourishing dish from a lush region of France, making use of many delicious local ingredients.

MATELOTE NORMANDE

This is a creamy dish from the rich dairy districts of Normandy in France. It is a good example of a dish making use of local ingredients. Use a mixture of white fish, including some eel. Serve with a garnish of triangular shaped croûtons and with some mushrooms sautéed in butter.

SERVES 6
1.6 kg [3½ lb] firm white fish
225 g [½ lb] conger eel
1 L [1 quart] mussels in shells
1 large onion
60 g [2½ oz] softened butter
850 ml [1½ pt] dry still cider
15 ml [1 tablespoon] freshly chopped parsley
50 g [2 oz] flour
30 ml [2 tablespoons] thick cream
chopped parsley to garnish

1 Remove skin and bones from all the fish. Cut the flesh into pieces about 10 cm [4"] in size.

2 Wash and scrub the mussels thoroughly. Discard any which are open.

3 Peel and chop the onion. Melt 15 g [½ oz] butter in a large flameproof casserole and fry the onion gently until soft and transparent.

4 Put the mussels into a saucepan with 175 ml [6 fl oz] of the cider. Cover the pan and heat gently until the mussels open.

5 Remove the pan from the heat. Pour the mussel liquor into the casserole. Remove the mussels from their shells, set aside and keep warm.

6 Add the parsley to the casserole and cook very gently for 5 minutes.

7 Pour in the remaining cider and 575 ml [1 pt] water and bring to the boil.

8 Add the fish, cover the casserole and bring back to simmering point. Simmer for 10 minutes.

9 Remove from the heat. Take out the fish, draining for one minute, over the casserole. Put the fish in a warmed shallow serving dish, and keep warm under buttered paper.

10 Mix the remaining butter and the flour to make a beurre manié and add this, in small spoonfuls, to the liquid in the casserole. Stir until the butter melts.

11 Replace the casserole over medium heat and bring to the boil, stirring. Stir until the sauce thickens slightly. Stir in the cream and remove from the heat.

12 Sprinkle the mussels on top of the fish and pour sauce over. Garnish.

BOURIDE

Even if we cannot make an authentic bouillabaisse, we can make a bouride which is very similar. Creamy and garlicky, it has the real southern flavour of its French home in Provence. You will need 275 ml [½ pt] homemade or bought egg-based mayonnaise. If you cannot find one of the fish listed, choose another variety of firm white fish.

SERVES 4-6

450 g [1 lb] each of fresh haddock, cod and rock salmon or halibut
salt
freshly ground black pepper
6 small slices of bread
45 ml [3 tablespoons] olive oil
1 garlic clove

For the fish stock:
700 g [1½ lb] fish heads, bones and trimmings from white fish
1 medium-sized onion
1 leek
50 ml [2 fl oz] white wine
20 ml [4 teaspoons] white wine vinegar
zest of orange quarter

For the garlic mayonnaise:
15 ml [1 tablespoon] fresh white breadcrumbs
15 ml [1 tablespoon] white wine vinegar
4 garlic cloves
275 ml [½ pt] mayonnaise
a few drops of lemon juice
salt and pepper
2 egg yolks

1 Remove any skin and bones from the fish and reserve for the stock. Cut the fish into 5 cm [2"] pieces and season. Refrigerate.

2 Make the fish stock. Peel and slice the onion and wash the leek and slice the white part. Put all the ingredients in a large saucepan with 850 ml [1½ pt] water. Bring to the boil. Skim well. Lower the heat so that the liquid just simmers. Half cover the pan and simmer for 30 minutes. Do not leave it for any longer.

3 While the stock is simmering, prepare the garlic mayonnaise. Mix the breadcrumbs into the vinegar. Leave to soak for 5 minutes. Drain and squeeze the crumbs dry in kitchen paper.

4 Peel and crush the garlic well. Mix it with the crumbs until blended to a smooth paste. Add, little by little, 15 ml [1 tablespoon] mayonnaise. Work it in with the back of a spoon to make a smooth cream.

5 Mix this garlic cream into the remaining mayonnaise. Sharpen the mayonnaise with lemon juice, and add salt and pepper to taste. Reserve.

6 Toast the slices of bread very lightly on both sides. Heat the olive oil in a frying-pan, over low heat. Fry the toast on both sides until well soaked with oil, and golden. Peel and cut the garlic clove in half. Rub over toast while still hot. Keep warm.

7 Strain the fish stock into a bowl. Squeeze as much stock as you can out of the solid matter. Discard the solids. Rinse out the pan and put back the liquid stock.

8 Bring the stock to simmering point. Add the pieces of fish with a large spoon. Simmer until the fish is firm, about 6–10 minutes. Do not overcook.

9 Remove the fish with a slotted spoon. Put it on a warmed serving dish. Keep it warm under buttered paper. Reserve the stock in the pan.

10 Measure 150 ml [¼ pt] garlic mayonnaise into a bowl. Put the rest into a sauce-boat, cover it and set aside.

11 Beat the egg yolks into the garlic mayonnaise and transfer to a saucepan.

12 Trickle the hot fish stock into the mayonnaise, stirring quickly all the time. Set over very low heat and stir until the mixture thickens slightly. Do not let it boil.

13 Check the seasoning of the garlic soup. Add extra lemon juice, salt and pepper if needed.

14 Strain the garlic soup into a hot tureen. Serve with the dish of fish, the garlic toast and the sauce-boat of mayonnaise.

Bouride is a very rich and creamy dish, strongly flavoured with garlic.

FISH AND 'CHIPS' CASEROLE

To casserole 'chips' sounds crazy, but these 'chips' are not fried potatoes, they are chipolatas! If you do not think fish and sausages go together, try this dish and see how delicious it is. Serve with baked potatoes and hot grilled tomatoes putting the potatoes in the oven well before the casserole. Fish cutlets or steaks should be used for this dish.

SERVES 4
4 cod or haddock cutlets, each 175 g [6 oz]
350 g [¾ lb] onions
175 g [6 oz] mushrooms
150 ml [¼ pt] tomato juice
dash of Worcestershire sauce
salt and pepper
5 ml [1 teaspoon] dried marjoram
4 cooked chipolata sausages

1 Heat the oven to 160°C [325°F] gas mark 3. Peel and chop the onions finely. Wipe and chop the mushrooms and put both the onions and mushrooms in the bottom of an ovenproof casserole.

2 Wipe the fish cutlets and lay them in a single layer on top of the vegetables in the casserole.

3 Mix the tomato juice with the Worcestershire sauce. Pour it into the casserole. Sprinkle the dish with salt and pepper, and the marjoram.

4 Cover the dish, and cook for 10 minutes. Cut the chipolata sausages into 1.25 cm [½"] slices. Add them to the casserole and continue cooking for 10–15 minutes until the fish is tender.

5 When the fish is ready, serve it hot from the casserole.

SPICY STAND-BY CASEROLE

A keen fisherman might be shocked, but frozen fish fillets in an unusual spicy sauce make a super stand-by for the busy cook. This casserole which has an Italian flavour about it is a joy, since you can make the store-cupboard sauce ahead of time and use the fillets still frozen. Use white fish such as coley, haddock or plaice. Serve with sautéed potatoes and a green salad.

SERVES 4
700 g [1½ lb] frozen white fish fillets
2 medium-sized onions
1 large garlic clove
15 ml [1 tablespoon] olive oil
30 ml [2 tablespoons] tomato purée
10 ml [2 teaspoons] ground cinnamon
4 bay leaves
salt and pepper

1 Peel and chop the onions and garlic. Heat the oil in a small flame-proof casserole. When hot, fry the onion and garlic until soft.

2 Stir in the tomato purée and the cinnamon. Add the bay leaves and 225 ml [8 fl oz] water and season well with salt and pepper. Bring to simmering point.

3 Simmer for 20 minutes, uncovered, to make a thick sauce. Remove the bay leaves.

4 Heat the oven to 180°C [350°F] gas mark 4. Lay the frozen fillets in 3 or 4 layers in the casserole. Spoon some of the hot sauce over them.

5 Cover the casserole. Put it in the oven for 20–30 minutes until the fish is white and flaky. Serve hot from the casserole.

MATELOTE ROUGE

Red wine is used here with white fish: it sounds and looks a little strange but the flavour is excellent. It is so good that the dish can be made wholly with the cheaper varieties of white fish but, if you feel extravagant, use 100–175 g [4–6 oz] firm fish such as trout or halibut in place of the cheaper fish. This version of a matelote is unusual in another way too; the fish pieces are fried to seal them instead of being put into hot liquid. Be generous with the fried croutons.

SERVES 4
600 g [1¼ lb] mixed fillets of cod, hake and whiting
75 g [3 oz] peeled prawns, fresh, or frozen and thawed
50 g [2 oz] seasoned flour
2 medium-sized onions
1 medium-sized carrot
575 ml [1 pt] dry red wine
1 sprig thyme

The combination in this recipe, red wine and fish, is rather strange but it offers an original and attractive variation.

1 sprig rosemary
15 ml [1 tablespoon] freshly
    chopped parsley
2 strips lemon zest
1 large garlic clove
salt and pepper
30 ml [2 tablespoons] oil
50 g [2 oz] butter
175 g [6 oz] button mushrooms

For the garnish:
5–6 slices white bread
15 ml [1 tablespoon] olive
    oil
30 ml [2 tablespoons] butter
50 g [2 oz] drained peeled
    prawns
30 ml [2 tablespoons] freshly
    chopped parsley

1 Skin the fish fillets and pat dry. Cut them into 2.5 cm [1"] pieces. Drain the prawns. Toss all the fish in the flour. Set aside.

2 Peel and chop one onion and slice the carrot. Put the wine, parsley, onion and carrot, herbs, lemon zest and peeled garlic into a large saucepan. Season with salt and pepper. Cover the pan, bring to simmering point, and simmer for 30 minutes.

3 When the pan is simmering safely, chop the second onion finely. Heat 25 g [1 oz] butter and the oil in another saucepan, which will hold all the ingredients. Fry the white fish and prawns, in batches, until just cooked through and golden, about 5 minutes.

4 Take out the last batch of fish and prawns. Put in the chopped onion. Add the remaining butter if necessary. Lower the heat, cover the pan, and cook very gently until the onion is just soft and golden but not browned.

5 Meanwhile, wipe and quarter the mushrooms. Add them to the pan. Cook very gently for 5 minutes with the pan uncovered and then remove from the heat.

6 Put the fish back in the pan on top of the onions and mushrooms. Strain the cooked wine sauce into the pan. Put over very low heat and simmer until the sauce reduces enough to be slightly thickened.

7 While the stew is simmering, make the garnish. Remove the crusts from the bread and cut each slice into 4 or 5 rounds. Heat the oil and butter in a frying-pan and fry the bread until golden. Remove from the pan and fry the prawns for 1 minute.

8 Turn the stew into 4 individual earthernware dishes or 1 large one. Lay the round croûtons over the stew and scatter on the prawns and parsley.

Flavourful fish

Here are more delicious ways of cooking fish, including main dishes and rare and interesting hors d'oeuvres. No special equipment is needed, no intricate techniques are involved, no time-consuming preparation is called for; just choose your fish and produce a variety of flavours from the naturally juicy to the unusually spicy. There's a dish for every occasion and every palate.

Explained in full detail are no less than four different methods of cooking fish, suitable for both oily and white fish.

The first three methods, oven poaching, braising and sousing, all involve cooking in the oven while the fourth, pickling, involves no cooking.

Oven poaching and braising are two straightforward and effective ways of cooking fish for main meals. Oven poaching is used for those cuts of fish which are not suitable for poaching on top of the cooker. Braising introduces vegetables to the baking dish which not only add flavour to the fish while cooking and help to keep it moist, but also improve the appearance of the finished dish by adding colour.

Both sousing and pickling involve the use of a marinade which softens the fish bones (which can be spiky) and imparts a distinctive flavour. The dishes are prepared in advance as many are at their best after 2–3 days' marinating. These methods are more suitable for oily fish as the marinade successfully counteracts the richness of the fish. Soused and pickled fish are generally served cold as an hors d'oeuvre or are made into a meal with salad vegetables in season and some fresh bread.

OVEN POACHING

Many of the principles discussed in connection with poaching fish on top of the cooker (see pages 41–51) apply also to oven poaching, as do the general principles (such as taking care to season well and not to overcook) which apply to all methods of cooking fish. Poaching on top of the cooker is particularly suitable for whole fish, fillets and smoked fish. Oven poaching is better suited to steaks and portions, and is also suitable for fillets.

However, oven poaching can be compared more readily, in practical terms, with baking. Oven temperatures and cooking times are the same for both processes. There are several automatic advantages when using the oven as opposed to the hob: fishy smells are kept to a minimum and service is straight from the baking dish. This means less handling of the fish and consequently less fear of it breaking up. It also means less washing-up.

The main difference between oven poaching and baking (and this is where the term poaching is justified and the association with poaching on top of the cooker comes in) is the use of liquid. Oven-poached fish is cooked in sufficient liquid to come half-way up the fish. A little less liquid is used than when poaching fish on top of the cooker as evaporation in the oven is very slight. After poaching, the liquid can be used to create some of the most delicious sauces.

When poaching prime quality fish such as sole or turbot the liquid used is usually fish fumet (see pages 44–45), dry white wine, dry vermouth or dry cider. Additions are by no means essential but you can use mildly flavoured additives, such as mushrooms, which will not mask the fine flavour of the fish.

When cooking less tasty fish, such as cod or mock halibut, the liquid can be more strongly flavoured with herbs and vegetables to enhance the flavour of both the fish and the sauce. The recipe for fillet of cod bretonne is a good example: the creamy vegetable sauce brings a little glamour to an otherwise ordinary fish.

BRAISING FISH

This is another method of oven cooking fish to be compared to, but

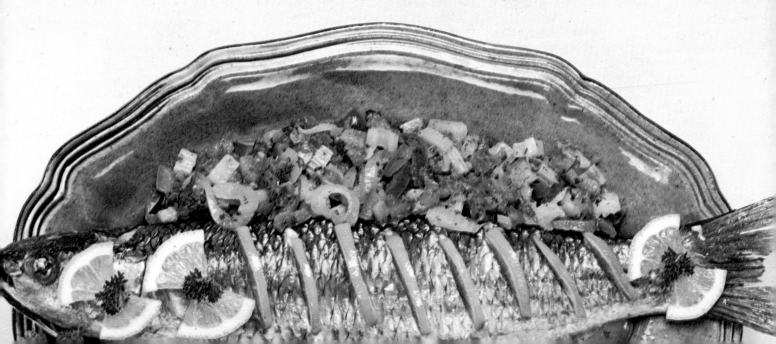

Grey mullet braised with vegetables is garnished with slices of lemon.

Dry white vermouth is an excellent fortified wine for poaching fish, especially in recipes calling for white wine and herbs. Its use can often avoid the opening of a bottle of wine just for cooking. It has a more pronounced flavour than white wine and can be used neat for extra flavour, or diluted with one-third as much water.

not confused with, baking. The cooking times and temperatures are the same but the results are different.

Braising is a method of cooking whole fish of a medium size, steaks or thick slices of fish on a bed of vegetables. The tougher cuts of meat are usually cooked in this way and the principles are basically the same for fish. The recipe given here which illustrates this method of cooking fish is grey mullet with lemon.

The fish is prepared in the same way as for any other method of cooking fish. Whole fish are laid raw on the bed of prepared vegetables. Fish steaks or slices need to be fried for a few minutes on each side in hot fat to seal the surfaces, before being laid on the vegetable bed.

The vegetables used are usually chosen from the following: onions, celery, leeks, carrots, peppers and tomatoes. The vegetables are cleaned and diced or finely sliced and are fried gently in butter to soften, before being spread over the base of the dish. Vegetables add both flavour and colour, and herbs such as bay leaves and garlic are often included too.

The vegetables are served with the fish as an integral part of the finished dish. For attractive presentation the cooked fish is usually transferred to a warmed serving platter and the vegetables arranged around the sides as a garnish.

The liquid which is added to the dish is normally fish stock or fish fumet (pages 44–45), white wine or cider. The amount is very small, just sufficient to cover the bed of vegetables, and is added cold. The dish is then covered tightly so that evaporation is minimal. If tomatoes are being used there is no need to use any liquid. Enough juice will run from the tomatoes as they cook to keep the

other vegetables and the fish moist.

By the end of braising time the liquid in the dish should be well flavoured. You may find you have too much, though. Serving fish swamped in liquid, however well-flavoured, looks unappetizing.

If there is too much liquid you can reduce it by rapid boiling, having first drained it off the vegetables and fish. This will not only improve the flavour and consistency but also the appearance of the finished dish. Alternatively, the liquid can be thickened by the addition of a little beurre manié. Again, the liquid is strained off and thickened on top of the cooker and then poured back over the fish and vegetables on the serving platter.

SOUSING AND PICKLING

Soused and pickled (sometimes called spiced) are the terms used to describe fish which has been marinated in an acid solution. This is one area of cooking where the terms are not clearly defined. In Britain, sousing means to cook the fish in the oven in an acid-based solution. The fish is then cooled and allowed to marinate in the cooking liquid. In Europe, the fish is usually cooked beforehand (either by frying or grilling) and is then immersed in the vinegar solution to marinate.

The British method of sousing is used for fish rich in oil such as herring and mackerel, rather than white fish as the acidity of the marinade ingredients offsets the richness of the fish giving it an appetizing, piquant flavour. The acid also softens the small bones in the fish and acts as a preservative. Fish soused by the British method should be eaten within three days.

A vinegar marinade is also used to pickle fresh herrings which have been lightly salted beforehand. With this method the fish is not cooked by heat at all. Instead of cooking the fish is simply cured by acid in the marinade. This process is an excellent way of preserving herrings and provides one of the best known pickled fish dishes—rollmops. If immersed in the marinade and kept refrigerated in an airtight jar, herrings will keep in perfect condition for several weeks.

The marinade
The ingredients of the marinade must be well balanced to produce a

pleasing dish and it is important that the mixture is not too harsh. The quantity should be sufficient to cover the fish generously.

In Britain, malt vinegar is more commonly used because of the brewing tradition which makes malt readily available. If it is too harsh, the vinegar can be used diluted, roughly one part water to three parts vinegar or up to half and half.

Vinegar is not always used and the marinade is then flavoured with dry wine or dry cider. The recipe given for soused mackerel is an example. The fish is cooked in the wine and then soused in the liquid resulting in a finer flavour.

Herbs, spices, sugar and vegetables are added to the marinade for flavouring. The herbs that are used include bay leaves, parsley, tarragon and fennel.

Step-by-step to

MAKES 8
8 fresh herrings
50 g [2 oz] coarse salt
550 ml [1 pt] white wine or
**   cider vinegar**
1 large onion

3 Drain fish. Lay skin side down on a board. Peel and slice onion. Cut gherkins in half lengthways.

Vegetables are used to add flavour when poaching cod fillets.

Cover and refrigerate until needed.

4 Wash, de-seed and finely chop the green pepper. Peel and finely slice the onion. Wash and finely slice the celery.

5 Heat the olive oil over medium heat in a flameproof casserole large enough to accommodate the fish.

6 When hot, fry the pepper, onion and celery together gently over low heat until they begin to soften.

7 Meanwhile, peel and chop the garlic. Peel, de-seed and chop the tomatoes and chop the parsley.

8 Add all these to the frying vegetables and cook gently for a minute or so. Season with salt and pepper.

9 Remove the casserole from the heat, lay the fish on top of the vegetables and baste it well. Tuck the bay leaf and thyme on either side of the fish and cover. (If you have no lid use oiled greaseproof paper.)

10 Braise in the centre of the oven for 30–40 minutes depending on size, basting several times. Test the fish after 30 minutes to see if it is cooked.

11 To serve, lay the whole fish on a hot serving plate and keep warm. Boil the vegetables rapidly, uncovered, until most of their juice has evaporated. Spoon the vegetables along either side of the fish.

SWEET PICKLED HERRINGS

Herring fillets pickled in this manner have a richer, sweeter and less acid flavour than traditional rollmops. Preparation must start the day before as, instead of being lightly salted in brine, the fish is filleted and salted overnight in pure salt. Make sure the herrings are really fresh when you buy them and clean and fillet them yourself (see pages 4–5) or ask the fishmonger to fillet them for you.

These pickled herrings, once refrigerated will keep for several months but are best eaten within a few weeks.

Serve the fillets either whole or cut into pieces and arranged in a dish with a garnish of the onion rings, a couple of fresh bay leaves and some sliced stuffed olives.

SERVES 6
3 large fresh herrings
block or coarse salt
150 ml [$\frac{1}{4}$ pt] distilled malt vinegar or wine vinegar
100 g [$\frac{1}{4}$ lb] granulated or soft brown sugar
25 g [1 oz] mixed pickling spice
1 large onion
2 bay leaves

1 Trim the fillets into a neat shape and remove all visible bones.

2 Layer the fillets flat into a glass or china dish, sprinkling each layer thickly with salt. Cover and refrigerate overnight.

3 Next morning, rinse the fillets thoroughly in cold running water, drain well and pat dry with kitchen paper. Wipe out the dish.

4 Put the vinegar, sugar and pickling spice into a saucepan with 150 ml [$\frac{1}{4}$ pt] water and bring slowly to the boil. Remove from the heat and allow to become cold.

5 Peel the onion and slice finely into rings. Layer the fillets and onion rings into the cleaned dish, or into a plastic box if you wish to store them.

6 Strain the cold spiced vinegar over the fillets (it should just cover them) and tuck the bay leaves down the sides.

7 Cover the dish and refrigerate for 8 hours before draining and using the fillets, or seal the box securely and store in the refrigerator.

A Friday fry-up

Crisp and golden and piping hot, fish and chips can make a very delicious meal. Here is explained how to fry fish to perfection, so that when the fish itself is cooked the coating is evenly browned and crisp. The method is popular all over the world; this course includes many well-known favourites like English fish and chips, Italian fritto misto and Japanese tempura.

It is much easier to achieve first class results by frying fish in deep rather than shallow fat. The temperature of the fat is so high and the cooking so rapid that, as the coating browns to perfection, the fish inside is cooked to just the right degree.

The fish itself is protected from direct contact with the hot fat by a substantial coating, yet it cooks rapidly because it is virtually surrounded by heat. The fat is really very hot, which means that immediately the coating touches the hot fat it sets, imprisoning all the juices and flavour of the fish. The coating browns quickly and evenly, less fat is absorbed, and the result is crispy, grease-free and succulent at the centre.

To deep fry successfully, however, you must have the right equipment and oils, the fish should be prepared correctly and cooked at an exact temperature. Care and attention are key words to successful deep frying.

THE FISH

Fish for frying, whether in shallow or deep fat, should not be more than 2.5 cm [1″] thick. It is important that the heat is able to penetrate and cook the fish in the time it takes to brown and crisp the coating. A burnt coating or undercooked fish will render the result inedible. As long as this rule is observed, the fish can be fried whole, in fillets or in chunks.

The fish can also be beaten with potato to make fish cakes. This is an ideal cooking method for cheaper, less flavoursome varieties of white fish, which can be cheered up with generous seasoning and rich, creamy potato. Fish cakes can also be shallow fried and a recipe is given on page 84.

As soon as you get the fish home, remove it from its wrappings, rinse under cold running water and drain thoroughly. Keep the fish chilled, covered with polythene or foil until needed.

The most suitable fish for deep frying is given below.

Small whole fish such as sprats, sardines, smelts, whitebait, portion-sized dabs, sole and plaice, and small shellfish, such as scampi, prawns and mussels.

Fillets of haddock, cod, whiting, coley and hake.

Chunks of large fish, such as halibut, turbot, brill and monk fish.

THE COATING

All fish for frying must be carefully and thoroughly enclosed in a coating which will protect it from the hot fat and seal in all its juices and flavour. The coating must be fairly substantial, in order to be effectively protective. Dipping fish in egg and then white breadcrumbs which have been dried in the oven is one way of coating the fish. The other is to use batter. There are many variations on a basic flour, water and oil batter (see right).

One exception is whitebait. These are so small and need such brief cooking that they are at their best simply lightly coated in seasoned flour. No further coating is necessary.

Egg and breadcrumbs

It is not necessary to measure the quantities for egg and breadcrumbing as the flour can be applied from a dredger and any breadcrumbs that

are left over can be put back into storage. If, though, you are coating small pieces of fish and a dredger is not very satisfactory, allow between 25–50 g [1–2 oz] for each 450 g [1 lb] fish.

Batter coatings

Batter is the most popular coating for deep frying fish. Batter cannot be shallow fried, whereas egg and breadcrumbed fish can. The batter must be sufficiently sticky to cling to the surfaces of the fish and not run off. To coat 450 g [1 lb] fish you will need up to 425 ml [¾ pt] fritter batter.

The batter that is used to coat fish for that traditional dish, fish and chips is plain fritter batter. For 425 ml [¾ pt] fritter batter, sift 100 g [¼ lb] plain flour with salt. Make a well in the centre and pour in 30 ml [2 tablespoons] oil and 150 ml [¼ pt] cold water. Draw flour in from the sides, mix until thick; leave for 30 minutes.

The batter is very easily lightened by adding beaten egg whites just before the batter is to be used. Use two egg whites for 425 ml [¾ pt] batter. The egg whites must be whisked to their maximum volume to ensure a light and crisp batter. This egg white batter makes a very satisfactory coating for all types of fish and the results are always much lighter than plain batter and particularly crisp and mouthwatering.

Batters for coating fish can be made even more light and airy by using a light alcoholic liquid, such as cider, beer or lager, in place of plain water in the batter mix. When an alcoholic liquid is used, the batter must be allowed to stand before it is used so that it can ferment and effervesce to lighten it. Beaten egg whites are always used in these batters.

Tempura batter is heavier than plain batter. Sift 100 g [¼ lb] plain flour with salt. Break one egg into another bowl and whisk in 15ml [1 tablespoon] soy sauce. Gradually add 150 ml [¼ pt] iced water. Add flour to the liquid 15 ml [1 tablespoon] at a time and whisk vigorously. This makes 275 ml [½ pt] batter. A recipe for tempura is given on page 76.

FATS FOR DEEP FRYING

To store the oil, after each frying session allow the oil to cool. Strain through a sieve lined with absorbent kitchen paper to remove sedi-

ments and bits of coating. Strain the oil again into a container with a tight fitting lid and store in a cool dark place. Never pour hot fat into a plastic container.

The best medium in which to deep fry fish is undoubtedly oil. There are various types of oil, some with a distinctive flavour, others with no flavour at all. The prices also vary enormously and, as a large quantity is needed, some of the prices are prohibitive.

Vegetable, nut or corn oil are best for deep frying as they reach frying temperature fairly quickly and, having a high smoke point, can be raised to the high temperature necessary for deep frying without burning. Lard and clarified dripping can also be used for deep frying but both burn easily at a lower temperature than oil and are, therefore, difficult to regulate.

Quantity of oil

Because of the danger element, it is unwise to fill a pan to more than one-third or a half full of oil. A fire can flare up instantly from fat bubbling over the sides of the pan if you are cooking on gas. It will also burn and smoke very unpleasantly on an electric cooker.

For safety's sake use no more than the quantities given here:
● for a pan 23 cm [9″] in diameter, 12.5 cm [5″] deep with a capacity of 4 L [7 pt] use 1.5–1.75 L [2½–3 pt] oil;
● for a pan 20 cm [8″] in diameter, 9cm [3¾″] deep with a capacity of 2.75 L [5 pt] use 1.2 L [2 pt] oil.

EQUIPMENT

The one piece of special equipment that is essential for deep frying is, of course, the pan. There are many types available nowadays, so pick one to suit your particular need. It is possible, if you do not possess a deep fat fryer, to use a heavy-based saucepan with a folding basket that is made to fit any pan. The basket is, in fact, only used for fish coated with egg and breadcrumbs as batter would stick to the mesh. The pan must be large enough to completely cover the source of heat and deep enough to take the required quantity of oil safely.

The easiest and most accurate way of testing the temperature of the fat is to use a frying thermometer. It is certainly worth investing in one if you

70

deep fry food regularly.

Lifting the fish out of the batter and into the fat is best done with a skewer. This means that no batter is scraped off and your hand is at a safe distance from the hot fat.

A perforated spoon is invaluable for lifting the fish out of the hot fat. It ensures that excess fat can drain back into the pan rather than be spooned out with the fish. With larger slices of fish it may be easier to use a fish slice.

Absorbent kitchen paper will efficiently complete the task of draining the fish.

THE METHOD

Far too many fires start in the kitchen with blazing fat pans, so make sure the pan is clean, the fat is heated slowly, the handle does not jut out over the cooker and there is no water about. Never carry a pan of hot oil.

Because frying is such a quick method of cooking, it is more than ever essential to be thoroughly organized with everything in its proper place. It is important not only to know exactly what you will need but also in what order.

Preliminary steps

Several things must be done before you contemplate actually frying the fish. The fish should already have been rinsed and chilled as soon as it was brought home from the fishmonger.

The first step, then, is to prepare the batter or breadcrumb coating. Make the batter, apart from adding the egg whites, and chill it until needed. For a breadcrumb coating, assemble the dredger of flour, the bowl of beaten egg and the breadcrumbs piled on a large sheet of greaseproof paper.

Preparing the fish

Small whole fish generally need to be topped and tailed and gutted. The gutting of round fish is described in detail on pages 4–5 and of flat fish on pages 26–27.

The exception here is whitebait, which is so small that it is fried and eaten, quite literally, whole. Whitebait is a very small silvery fish. It is the small fry of herring and sprats. As to when a whitebait becomes a sprat, the unofficial definition is when it is large enough to need gutting and beheading before it is cooked.

The fish can be cleaned (gutted) in advance, lightly seasoned and stored, chilled, until needed. However, the cleaning of fish is best done as near cooking time as possible, and with a tasty coating the preliminary seasoning is not so important.

Mussels are prepared as described on pages 124–125 and are then shaken in a pan over gentle heat until they open. They are then removed from their shells. Discard any mussels which remain closed. The preparation and cooking of other small shellfish are described on pages 87–91.

Fillets of fish, if small enough, can simply be wiped over with a damp cloth, seasoned if wished and kept chilled if not needed immediately. If they are too thick for frying, the fillets can be cut into portions 150–175 g [5–6 oz] in weight and not more than 2.5 cm [1″] thick.

Chunks or pieces of fish can be cut from fillets, steaks and cutlets. It is important that the chunks be boneless as it is difficult to locate and remove bones inside a piece of fish that has been coated, and coming across one inadvertantly could ruin the enjoyment of the dish. The chunks or pieces should not be much larger than bite sized.

Before the fish is coated with batter, it is given a light dusting of seasoned flour. Shake well to dislodge surplus flour. This should be applied just before the fat is heated so that the flour does not have time to absorb moisture from the fish and become soggy.

An egg and breadcrumb coating can be applied now, rather than after the fat has been heated, as it is quite a long operation and hot fat cannot be kept waiting.

All accompaniments and garnishes should be ready to be served before you start frying. Heat all the serving dishes and plates so that the fish will not be cooled when it is served. Keep vegetables, serving dishes and plates hot in the oven while frying the fish.

Arrange some crumpled kitchen paper on a baking tray ready to drain the fish. This can be put into the oven to keep the first batch of fish hot while the rest is being fried.

Heating the oil

It is exceedingly important that the fat is at the right temperature for frying before the fish is lowered into the pan. It must be hot enough to seal the coating on contact. Fat that is too cool will soak into the coating and the result will be unappetizing.

The best temperature varies a little with different oils and also with the nature and size of the pieces of fish. Recommended temperatures can, therefore, only be guidelines. The usual temperature is between 180°C [350°F] and 195°C [380°F], the lower temperature being for larger portions of fish needing a slightly longer time for the heat to penetrate and the higher temperature for small pieces of fish needing brief cooking.

Pour the correct quantity of fat carefully into the pan with the basket in position if you are using a breadcrumb coating. Remove the basket and put it away if you are using a batter coating. Put the pan over low heat, stand the thermometer in it, and heat very gently to the correct frying temperature.

Finishing the batter

While the oil is heating you will have time to finish the batter. Keep a very careful watch over the pan of oil and on no account leave the kitchen.

Whisk the egg whites to their maximum volume and fold lightly into the chilled batter mixture. Put the batter into a deep bowl so that the pieces of fish can be entirely immersed and evenly coated all over. Put the bowl on a firm surface near the cooker.

The oil will probably have reached frying temperature during this time. If you do not have a thermometer, drop a small chip of raw potato into the pan from the end of a spoon. Moderate

bubbling means that the fat is hot enough, but not too hot, for frying.

Coating the fish with batter

When frying temperature is reached you can start coating the fish with batter. Dip the fish, one or two pieces at a time, into the batter. Make sure all the surfaces are evenly coated. Lift out on a skewer, one at a time, holding briefly over the bowl to allow excess batter to drip back. Immediately transfer the pieces of fish to the pan of oil, one at a time, lowering each piece gently into the hot oil. Skewers are particularly use-

ful here, as they can safely be dipped into the hot fat, whereas fingers cannot!

Breadcrumbed fish should be put into the basket with a skewer or tongs and the basket lowered slowly into the fat.

Fry as many pieces as the pan will take comfortably. Do not overcrowd the pan or the temperature of the fat will be lowered. In a pan containing 1.5–1.75 L [2½–3 pt] oil do not attempt to fry more than three portion-sized pieces of fish at one time.

Fry the fish until the coating is crisp and golden brown and the fish cooked through. This will take between 1½-5 minutes, depending on the size and thickness of the pieces. Turn once with a perforated spoon or skewer to brown both sides evenly.

Lift out the battered fish with a perforated spoon or fish slice, hold over the pan momentarily to drain, then lay on the crumpled paper on the baking tray. Breadcrumbed fish can be lifted out in the basket and transferred to the baking tray with tongs. Put the baking tray in the oven to keep hot while the remaining fish is fried.

When all the fish is fried, transfer it to a hot serving dish which can be lined with a paper doily. Serve piping hot, handing vegetables and a piquant sauce or wedges of lemon separately.

FRIED WHITEBAIT

Despite the fact that they are eaten whole, complete with heads and eyes, you have only to try this uniquely English delicacy to become addicted. Crispness is the all important quality, and frying whitebait in deep fat is the best way to achieve it. Because they are so small and fry so quickly, a higher fat temperature is used than for larger portions of fish. Choose very fresh whitebait (the fish should separate easily and not stick together), and handle the fish as little as possible to avoid bruising or crushing. Have everything for the meal ready before you start to prepare the fish because, once coated with flour, it should be fried and eaten without delay. Quick-frozen whitebait can give as good a result as fresh, but allow time for the fish to defrost thoroughly before cooking. Serve fried whitebait as a first course with plenty of lemon to squeeze over and some fresh brown bread and butter to eat with the fish. The fish will be at its best while hot.

SERVES 4
**450 g [1 lb] whitebait, fresh or
defrosted
45 ml [3 tablespoons]
seasoned flour
1.2–1.75 L [2–3 pt] oil
salt
cayenne pepper (optional)**

**For the garnish:
parsley sprigs
lemon wedges**

1 Start heating the pan of fat. Heat the oven to 180°C [350°F] gas mark 4.

2 Put the whitebait into a colander and submerge gently in cold water. Remove any foreign matter such as pieces of weed, if any. Drain well and pat dry with kitchen paper.

3 Spread the flour on a large piece of greaseproof paper and put the fish, a few at a time, in the centre. Lift the edges of the paper so that the fish roll over until lightly coated with flour and are quite separate from each other.

4 Transfer fish to a sieve and shake gently to dislodge surplus flour. Repeat until all fish are well coated. Put some crumpled kitchen paper on a baking tray.

5 When the oil reaches a temperature of 195°C [380°F] lower the basket, containing not more than a handful of whitebait, into the fat. Fry for 1 to 2 minutes, until the fish is very crisp and golden, shaking the basket now and then to prevent the fish clinging together.

6 Lift the basket out of the fat, drain over the pan for a few seconds, then turn the whitebait on to kitchen paper to drain, and keep hot in the oven.

7 Repeat with successive batches of whitebait, checking that the fat has returned to frying temperature before adding a fresh batch.

8 When all are fried, sprinkle with salt and a light sprinkling of cayenne pepper as well.

9 Line a hot serving dish with a plain paper doily and pile the whitebait into it. Garnish with lemon and parsley and serve at once.

SOLE COLBERT

⬚ *This classic dish is not difficult to cook provided you remember to measure the diameter of your frying basket before buying the fish! You need one small sole, complete with head and tail, for each person. It is fried flat, hence the need to check that the fish will fit into your frying basket.*

Although Dover sole is the traditional fish for this recipe because of its firm texture and fine flavour, lemon sole and dab are also delicious cooked this way and considerably less expensive. As you can fry only one fish at a time it is not a dish to undertake for more than a few people. If the worst happens and the fish is, after all, a little too big for the pan, try cutting off its tail. If it is then still too large, look for a wider pan which is still sufficiently deep and use a fish slice and palette knife to lift the fish in and out, instead of a frying basket.

Again, prepare the garnish in advance and have the plates heating in the oven. Making lemon butterflies is simple but effective. The Colbert butter can be made well in advance and refrigerated until needed.

SERVES 4
**4 sole, each weighing about
 250–350 g [9–12 oz]
2 medium-sized eggs
100 g [¼ lb] dried white
 breadcrumbs
a dredger of seasoned flour
1.2–1.75 L [2–3 pt] oil**

For the Colbert butter:
**100 g [¼ lb] unsalted butter
60 ml [4 tablespoons] finely
 chopped fresh parsley
10 ml [2 teaspoons] finely
 chopped fresh tarragon
30 ml [2 tablespoons] lemon
 juice
15 ml [1 tablespoon] meat jelly
 from underneath beef
 dripping
salt
freshly ground black pepper**

For the garnish:
**sprigs of parsley
lemon butterflies**

1 To make the Colbert butter, cream the butter until soft, then beat in the herbs, the lemon juice little by little, the meat jelly and salt and pepper to taste. Form into a roll about 2 cm [¾"] in diameter, wrap in greaseproof paper and chill in the refrigerator until needed.

2 If the fishmonger has not already done so, remove the dark skin of the sole (see pages 26–27) and trim the tail, small fins and edges of the fish. Rinse the fish and pat dry.

3 With a sharp knife make an incision right along the backbone on the skinned side of each fish.

4 Slide the knife under the flesh and ease the fillets away from the bone, leaving them attached at the head, tail and outer edge only, thus forming a large 'pocket' on each side of the backbone and freeing the bones.

5 Using scissors, cut through the backbone at the head and tail and in the middle. The purpose of this is to make it easier to remove the bone after frying.

6 Break the eggs into a flat dish, add 15 ml [1 tablespoon] water and beat lightly to mix.

7 Spread the breadcrumbs on a large piece of greaseproof paper.

8 Coat each sole with seasoned flour from the dredger, then with beaten egg and finally with breadcrumbs.

9 Press the breadcrumbs on firmly with a palette knife. If time allows, cover the fish loosely with greaseproof paper and leave in a cool place for about half an hour for the coating to firm up.

10 Cover a flat baking sheet with crumpled kitchen paper ready to drain the fish. Heat the oven to 180°C [350°F] gas mark 4.

11 When ready to fry, heat the fat, with the frying basket in position, to 190°C [375°F].

12 Raise the frying basket, put in one fish, cut side uppermost, and lower gently into the fat. Fry for about 3–4 minutes until golden and cooked through.

13 Lift out the basket, drain for a moment over the pan, and then gently lift out the fish with a slice and lay on the crumpled paper to drain.

14 Using a sharp knife, ease out and discard the back bone with the bones attached on either side. Keep the fish hot in the oven while frying the other fish.

15 While the last fish is frying, cut the Colbert butter into thin rounds.

16 Immediately before serving, insert several pieces of Colbert butter into the long central slit along the top of each fish. Garnish with sprigs of parsley and lemon butterflies. Serve immediately.

FISH AND CHIPS

For many people, juicy fish encased in a crisp golden batter and served with a pile of rustling, crisp potato chips, is an unbeatable combination. Everyone needs to know how to cook a creditable version of this British speciality and how to avoid the pitfalls of soggy, pallid chips and pale, flannelly fish. Chips are fried once until soft and again at a higher temperature.

Although a heavier batter makes the portions larger, a light, crisp batter is infinitely more pleasant to eat. Use 425 ml [¾ pt] plain fritter batter (see recipe on page 70); make this in advance and chill it. The optional egg whites will be added at a later stage. Keep them in a small container at room temperature until needed.

Boneless portions of almost any kind of white fish are suitable; chunky portions of cod, haddock, coley, rock salmon, hake or whiting are more traditional than fillets of flat fish, but there are no hard fast rules.

Serve with a piquant tartare sauce or a freshly made tomato sauce and wedges of lemon.

SERVES 3
3 fish fillets, each weighing about 175 g [6 oz]
1.2–1.75 L [2–3 pt] oil
seasoned flour in a dredger
700 g [1½ lb] raw chipped potatoes
2 large egg whites
425 ml [¾ pt] plain fritter batter

1 Fill a deep pan one-third to a half full of oil with the basket in position. Put in a thermometer and put pan to heat gently. Heat the oven to 180°C [350°F] gas mark 4.

2 Meanwhile, coat the fish lightly with seasoned flour, shaking to dislodge excess flour. Set aside.

3 When frying temperature for the potatoes is reached, remove the basket from the pan, put in the chips and lower the basket slowly into the hot fat.

4 Fry the chips at 180°C [350°F] for 5 minutes. Drain on absorbent kitchen paper then fry them again at 200°C [400°F].

5 While the chips are frying, finish the batter. Whisk the egg whites to their maximum volume and fold them into the prepared plain fritter batter. Transfer to a deep bowl and place it near the cooker.

6 When the chips are ready transfer them to some crumpled kitchen paper on a baking tray and keep them hot in the oven.

7 Make sure the oil is at the correct temperature for frying fish. It should not be more than 180°C [350°F].

8 When frying temperature is reached, submerge a piece of fish in the batter, lift out with a skewer, drain momentarily over the bowl and lower gently into the hot oil.

9 Repeat the process with the other pieces of fish. Have some crumpled kitchen paper ready for draining.

10 Fry until the batter is crisp and golden and the fish cooked through, about 3–5 minutes depending on thickness.

11 Lift the fish out with a skewer, drain over the pan for a moment and transfer to crumpled kitchen paper to drain.

12 Place each portion on a hot plate and add a portion of hot chips.

Sole is fried whole for this classic dish and garnished with Colbert butter.

JAPANESE TEMPURA

Tempura is a traditional Japanese way of cooking and serving food. The food is chosen for contrast in colour, flavour and texture and each Japanese cook will vary the ingredients according to taste, using eel, snapper, prawns, plaice, crab, flounder, scallops, squid, cod, green pepper, aubergine, lotus root, bamboo shoot and cauliflower. The food is fried in a special tempura batter (see page 70) which gives a particularly golden coating, and dipped in a soy-based sauce. Unlike plain fritter batter, the tempura batter must be used as soon as it is made. Remember to put the water into the refrigerator in advance to cool. The preparation of mussels is described on pages 124–125. The sauce must be made the day before.

The nicest way to serve tempura is from a fondue pot. The guests can then fry the food themselves and will appreciate the selection chosen. The food can just as easily be battered and fried in the kitchen by the hostess and served on a large serving dish.

The exotically named fuji foo yong is simply stuffed mushrooms which are battered and fried with the other vegetables.

Tempura would obviously, in Japan, be served with other Japanese dishes. Suitable accompaniments outside Japan would be a selection of salads, and fried rice.

SERVES 4
12 peeled fresh prawns
12 fresh mussels
4 spring onions
12 French beans
12 mange-tout
4-8 parsley sprigs
425 ml [¾ pt] tempura batter
1.2-1.75 L [2-3 pt] oil

For the tempura sauce:
1 small fresh ginger root
225 ml [8 fl oz] soy sauce
90 ml [6 tablespoons] granulated sugar
juice of half a lime or lemon
225 ml [8 fl oz] dry sherry
225 ml [8 fl oz] vegetable stock

For the fuji foo yong:
1 dried black mushroom

6 fresh peeled prawns
3 fresh or canned water chestnuts
2 spring onions
75 g [3 oz] bean sprouts
8 large flat mushrooms
1 small piece fresh ginger root
salt

For the garnish:
lemon wedges
parsley sprigs

1. To make the tempura sauce, finely slice the ginger root. Combine the ginger, soy sauce, sugar, lime or lemon juice, sherry and stock in a screw top jar. Leave to stand overnight.

2. Place the prawns on a board and score across the underside to prevent them curling up when fried.

3. Scrub mussels in several changes of water, remove beards, put in a large pan and shake over fierce heat until they open. Remove from the shells and discard the shells and any mussels that do not open.

4. Trim ends of the spring onions, green beans and mange-toute. Wash the parsley sprigs.

Japanese tempura is a colourful mixture of food including bean sprouts, mushrooms and prawns.

5. Arrange the prawns, mussels and vegetables on a plate and chill until ready to use.

6. To make the fuji foo yong, place the dried mushroom in a mixing bowl and pour over enough boiling water to barely cover. Leave until soft—about 15 minutes.

7. Dice the prawns. If using fresh water chestnuts peel them. Cut chestnuts into thin slices and cut the slices into thin strips.

8. Trim and finely chop the spring onions.

9. If canned bean sprouts are used, rinse them before chopping lightly.

10. Drain and chop the dried mushroom.

11. Wipe clean the fresh mushrooms. Remove and finely chop the stalks.

12. Grate the ginger.

13. Combine all the ingredients for the fuji foo yong, except the fresh mushroom caps, in a mixing bowl and season with salt.

14 Fill each cap with the mixture, arrange on the plate with the rest of the tempura ingredients and keep chilled.

15 Fill a deep fat fryer one-third full of oil. Heat to 180°C [350°F]. Heat the oven to 180°C [350°F] gas mark 4 and put a large serving dish and plates to warm.

16 Meanwhile, make the tempura batter following the instructions on page 70.

17 Dip individual pieces of food into the batter and transfer immediately to the hot fat.

18 Deep fry in small batches, turning once or twice until golden brown. Drain and keep hot on crumpled kitchen paper in the oven. Pour the sauce from the jar into four individual bowls.

19 Serve the fried food on a large serving dish garnished with wedges of lemon and parsley sprigs with an individual bowl of sauce for each diner.

FRITTO MISTO DI MARE

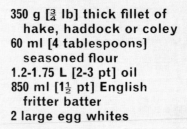

Under this name, but with local variations according to the region, restaurants all around Italy's coast serve the most delectable mixtures of fried fish. The fish used varies according to the local catch and the season and is often an ingenious way of making use of the little fish that are too small for other purposes. There should be at least three different kinds of fish and shellfish, preferably more, providing if possible a variety of shapes. A typical Italian mixture might include prawns or scampi, rings of previously boiled squid, small whole fish and bite-sized cubes of fish fillet from larger species. The important points are that the fish must be very fresh, the coating light, and the frying oil hot enough to crisp and brown the coating rapidly. Fry similar-sized fish together in a batch, so that the frying time and temperature can be adjusted to suit the size of the pieces.

The coating can be either egg and breadcrumbs or an egg white batter. Make the batter in advance and chill, but do not add the egg whites. A sharp, piquant sauce is always served with the fish, and instead of the customary mayonnaise-based tartare sauce you may prefer a less rich version made with hardboiled eggs and cream.

SERVES 4
24 cooked prawns
8 small whole fish, such as sardines, smelts or sprats
350 g [¾ lb] thin fillets of sole, plaice or dab

350 g [¾ lb] thick fillet of hake, haddock or coley
60 ml [4 tablespoons] seasoned flour
1.2-1.75 L [2-3 pt] oil
850 ml [1½ pt] English fritter batter
2 large egg whites

For the garnish:
lemon wedges
orange wedges
fresh parsley sprigs

1 Shell the prawns if necessary.

2 Cut the heads off the small whole fish.

3 Cut the thin fillets into 2.5 cm [1"] wide diagonal strips.

4 Skin the thick fillets if necessary and cut into 2.5 cm [1"] cubes.

5 Toss each variety of fish separately in seasoned flour and shake in a sieve to remove surplus flour.

6 Heat the oven to 180°C [350°F] gas mark 4 and put a large serving dish and plates to heat.

7 Pour the oil into the pan and put to heat slowly to 190°C [375°F].

8 Whisk the egg whites stiffly and fold gently but thoroughly into the chilled batter. Transfer to a deep bowl.

9 Cover a baking sheet with crumpled kitchen paper

10 Arrange the fish in separate piles, according to size.

11 Dip the pieces of fish in the batter on the end of a skewer and transfer to hot fat, briefly frying each batch separately. Check that the fat has regained frying temperature before frying each batch. The smaller pieces will need 1-2 minutes, and the larger pieces 3 minutes at the most.

12 Drain, and keep hot in the oven until all are fried.

13 Line the serving dish with a paper doily and pile fish in it in groups. Garnish with lemon and orange wedges and parsley sprigs.

MONK FISH 'SCAMPI'

Since it was discovered that the tail meat of a monk fish can be cut up into small pieces and fried to make a very good imitation scampi, the demand for it has increased. You might be lucky enough to find some in a local fish shop or market, especially if you live on the coast. Although no longer cheap, it is still good value for money because there is no wastage. It provides a mock 'scampi' which will deceive all but the experts and at roughly half the cost.

Remember to have the garnish and the accompaniments ready before starting to fry the fish. The three sauces are optional but delicious. If you are pressed for time when preparing the meal, the fish can be coated in advance, as it needs to rest for at least an hour to firm up. This quantity is enough to serve 4 as a starter, 2-3 as a main course.

SERVES 3-4
450 g [1 lb] tail piece of monk fish
15 ml [1 tablespoon] seasoned flour
2 small eggs
100 g [¼ lb] dried white breadcrumbs
1.2-1.75 L [2-3 pt] oil

For the garnish
fresh parsley sprigs
wedges of lemon

To serve:
thin slices of brown bread and butter
275 ml [½ pt] rémoulade tartare sauce or mayonnaise verte

1 Cut the fish into small pieces about 4 × 1.2 cm [1½ × ½"] and 1.2 cm [½"] thick. You should have about 30 pieces.

2 Put the seasoned flour on a piece of greaseproof paper and place next to the fish.

3 Break the eggs into a shallow dish, add 10 ml [2 teaspoons] water and beat lightly with a fork to mix well. Place next to the flour.

4 Pile the dried breadcrumbs on a large piece of greaseproof paper and place next to the bowl of beaten egg.

5 Have a clean board or flat tray available on which to collect the coated fish until you are ready to fry it.

6 Put a few pieces of fish at a time into the flour and lift the edges of the paper to coat them.

7 Using tongs, lift out each piece of fish in turn, shake lightly so that surplus flour falls back on to the paper, and lower the fish into the beaten egg.

8 Coat each piece of fish with the beaten eggs and dried white breadcrumbs. Sift any remaining breadcrumbs and put back into storage.

9 When all the pieces of fish are coated, cover loosely with greaseproof paper and leave for an hour to firm up.

10 When ready to fry, heat the oven to 180°C [350°F] gas mark 4 and put some crumpled kitchen paper on a baking tray.

11 Heat a pan one-third to a half full of oil, with the basket in position, until a thermometer registers 190°C [375°F].

12 Lift out the basket and carefully place about a quarter of the fish pieces in it.

13 Lower the basket gently into the fat and fry for 1-2 minutes until the coating turns golden brown and becomes crisp.

14 Immediately lift out the basket, drain over the pan for a second or two, then tip the fish on to the crumpled paper to drain. Put into the oven to keep hot.

15 Check that the fat has regained frying temperature, then fry the next batch of fish—and transfer to the oven in the same manner.

16 When all the pieces of fish are fried and drained, pile them on a hot, shallow doily-lined serving dish, garnish with the parsley and lemon and serve at once. The sauce should be served separately.

Variations

●For goujons, little strips of crispy fried fish, you can use any thin fillets, such as lemon sole, plaice, dab or megrim. They are often made from sole and, naturally, the finer the fish the better the flavour. Skin any dark-skinned fillet (see pages 4–5) and rub over with half a lemon. A little of the juice can be squeezed on to the fish. Cut each quarter-cut fillet on the diagonal into 2.5 cm [1"] strips. Coat with flour, egg and breadcrumbs, fry in oil, drain and serve as above.
●For mock whitebait, instead of 2.5 cm [1"] strips, cut the fillet into very thin strips, 8 mm [⅓"] wide. The very slender goujons which result make a good substitute for whitebait.

Frying tonight

Frying is a particularly quick and attractive way of cooking all types of lean white fish and small, whole oily fish. The white fish loses its often rather bland appearance and gains a deliciously crisp and golden surface which contrasts with its fragile flesh. Prime quality fish can be served simply with wedges of lemon—the basis of some classic dishes. Cheaper but equally wholesome varieties can be fried and served with many delicious sauces.

The principles of shallow frying fish in an open pan are the same as those for shallow frying meat, in fat and relatively quickly. The main difference between frying meat and frying fish is that fish is more fragile, which means that the fat is used at a slightly lower temperature and the food must be handled with greater care. A fish slice is an essential piece of equipment for lifting and turning the fish. Almost invariably, the fish is coated before frying. Frying is carried out in an open pan to ensure a crisp coating. There are many different coatings which can be used for fish and there is a list of several on page 80 which are suitable.

THE FISH

Fish for shallow frying should not be more than 2.5 cm [1″] thick. The following are the most suitable types:
small, whole flat fish such as dabs, plaice, sole, megrim and witch

small, whole oily fish such as trout, mackerel, herrings and sardines
fillets of sole, plaice, whiting, John Dory and mackerel
steaks and cutlets of cod, hake, halibut, turbot, brill and mock halibut.

Preparing the fish

Fish should always be removed from their wrappings as soon as possible, rinsed under cold running water and drained thoroughly. Keep the fish chilled, lightly covered with poly-thene or foil until needed.

While a fishmonger will always clean a whole fish for you, you can, of course, do this yourself. The process is described fully on pages 4–5 for round fish and on pages 26–27 for flat fish. The cleaning is, in fact, best done as near cooking time as possible. Once cleaned, the fish can be seasoned although, if being coated in seasoned flour, this is not strictly necessary.

Fillets of fish, steaks and cutlets can simply be wiped with a damp cloth, seasoned if wished and kept covered and chilled until needed.

The special preparation necessary for frying fish is to give it a coating to protect the delicate flesh from the intense heat of the fat and, at the same time, to add an attractive crispy surface. The softer the fish, the greater the need for a really protective coating which will set firmly on contact with hot fat.

SUITABLE COATINGS

Food that is to be fried is often given a coating to help retain the juices and flavour within the food. This protects the food from the intense heat of the fat and also stops it from absorbing an unnecessary amount of fat. A coating makes the food easier to handle, especially soft food such as fish, and gives it an attractive contrasting texture of a crisp, golden skin.

The coatings listed below are all very successful when used with fish. If you feel adventurous, experiment with different coating ingredients.

Flour, fine oatmeal and matzo meal are suitable for fillets, steaks and cutlets and small whole fish. The fish should be thoroughly dried before being rolled completley in the well-seasoned flour or the meal. A firmer coating can be achieved if, after being floured, the fish is dipped in milk, drained and given a second coating of flour.

Egg and breadcrumbs give a firmer, crisper and more protective coating than flour. Adding grated cheese or herbs to the breadcrumbs gives extra flavour.

Coarse oatmeal and rolled oats make attractive coatings for oily fish, particularly herrings. The flavour is improved if the oatmeal is first crisped in the oven or shaken in a pan over heat for a few minutes.

Crushed potato crisps and corn-flakes make rough-textured coatings, particularly good for fish cake mixtures.

Packet stuffing mixtures make readily available, easy to apply, useful coatings for less tasty fish.

FAT FOR SHALLOW FRYING

The fats used for shallow frying fish are butter, dripping and oil. The flavour of the fat is important when frying fish; butter and oil, mixed half and half, are very satisfactory. As with frying meat, it is customary in some recipes to use butter alone. To prevent the butter from burning it should first be clarified; melt and strain the butter through a muslin-lined sieve. Fish which is prepared a la meunière' is always fried in clarified butter. If you are using oil alone, olive oil has a distinctive flavour, but many people prefer the cleaner, less noticeable taste of vegetable oil.

The temperature of the fat

Fish needs more gentle treatment than meat and the temperature of the fat is, therefore, not quite so high. It must, though, be sufficient to seal and crisp the coating.

Oil and butter or butter alone: put in the fish while the butter is still foaming and maintain a steady heat so that the fish sizzles gently and the butter does not burn.

Oil alone or clarified dripping: heat the fat until a small cube of bread dropped in turns brown in 30 seconds. This heat is correct for thin fillets but for thicker pieces of fish such as steaks allow the temperature to drop slightly before lowering in the fish. The slightly lower temperature is needed so that the heat can penetrate to the centre of the fish without overbrowning the surface.

FRYING

Put 60 ml [4 tablespoons] butter and oil mixed into a large, heavy-based frying-pan. Heat gently until frying temperature is reached. While the butter is still foaming, lower in the fish, one at a time, skin side up. The fish should lie flat, with a small space between each one. Always allow the fat to regain frying temperature before lowering in the next piece. When frying in batches, do this between each batch.

Fry the fish until golden brown and turn once to brown the other side. To turn the fish, slide a fish slice under the fish and use a palette knife or spoon to hold it steady.

Frying times: allow two to three minutes each side for thin pieces of fish, and four to five minutes each side for whole fish and pieces 1.25-2.5 cm [½-1"] thick.

DRAINING AND SERVING

Like all fried food, fish should be well drained on crumpled kitchen paper and must always be served piping hot. Fish which is served in a sauce or dressing made from the pan juices is, obviously, not drained.

Remember to heat serving dishes in advance and have the garnishes and accompaniments prepared so that there is no delay in serving.

GARNISHES AND SAUCES

Vegetable garnishes are served with the fish primarily to add colour and

succulence. The vegetables are cooked briefly after the fish has been prepared and coated, but before it is fried. In this way, the vegetables are ready to serve immediately the fish is cooked. Once cooked, they are kept warm while the fish is being fried and are spooned over the fish just before serving. The vegetables that are most suitable are the more moist varieties, such as tomatoes, onions, mushrooms, celery and leeks.

Fried fish is enhanced by the sharp contrast of piquant flavours. Not without reason, lemon juice is the classic companion of fried fish. For a change, try lime juice or orange juice.

Sauces should be well flavoured

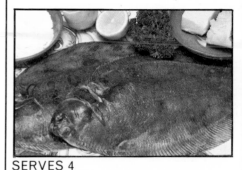

SERVES 4

2 sole, each weighing about 500 g [18 oz]
30 ml [2 tablespoons] seasoned flour
50 g [2 oz] clarified butter
50 g [2 oz] butter
10 ml [2 teaspoons] lemon juice
15 ml [1 tablespoon] freshly chopped parsley

4 Fry gently over medium heat until golden, 3–4 minutes. Turn carefully and fry until golden.

and spicy or piquant. Fish sauces can be either hot or cold. For hot sauces, try melted butter sauce, anchovy butter sauce, egg sauce, mushroom sauce, dill sauce, beetroot sauce, mustard sauce or cucumber sauce. Cold sauces include the favourite mayonnaise-based tartare sauce, walnut sauce, almond sauce or mayonnaise curry sauce. Experiment with different ingredients and flavourings for an individual sauce.

MARINATING

Marinating in a piquant dressing is an excellent way to impart flavour and variety to some of the less tasty varieties of fish. Lemon juice or vinegar is used for its acidity and herbs, garlic, spices, onions, anchovies and vegetables for extra flavour. This is a popular method in Europe and in the Middle East, where the fish is marinated sometimes before and sometimes after frying or grilling.

Fish marinated before cooking is more often served hot, with a little of the marinade spooned over just before serving. Fish marinated after cooking is served cold and makes an unusual first course.

Almost any firm-fleshed fish, both oily and white, is suitable for marinating: small fish can be cleaned and left whole but larger fish are better filleted, sliced, or cut into strips.

FRYING FROZEN FISH

Commercially frozen fish products usually carry full instructions and cooking times on the pack. Frozen fish is best cooked from the near frozen state, preferably within half an hour of being taken from the freezer. It is better coated, and the slight softening of the surface as the fish defrosts helps the coating to adhere more firmly.

Cook the fish in exactly the same way as fresh fish, allowing half as long again on each side.

Step-by-step to frying fish à la meunière

1 Fillet fish into quarter-cut fillets (see pages 26–27). Skin dark-skinned fillets. Rinse, pat dry.

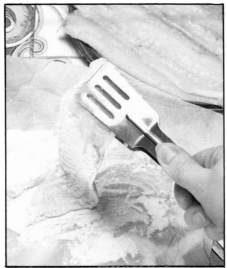

2 Spread seasoned flour on greaseproof paper. Press fillets into flour. Shake off surplus.

3 Heat clarified butter in large frying-pan. While butter foams, lower in four fillets.

5 Arrange fillets, overlapping, on a hot dish. Keep hot. Fry remaining fillets and transfer to dish.

6 Wipe out frying-pan and heat fresh butter rapidly, watching it carefully, until golden brown.

7 Pour butter promptly over fish, followed by the lemon juice. Scatter on the parsley and serve.

MARINATED ROCK SALMON

⊠⊠⊠*Italians are very keen on marinating fish, either before or after cooking. Rock salmon is an inexpensive, firm-fleshed fish usually sold skinned and filleted. Any firm-fleshed fish cut into small pieces can be used—Italians like filleted fresh sardines cooked in this way. In Italy, the fish would be served with a green salad and fresh bread, but sautéed potatoes and a fresh green vegetable would be equally appropriate.*

SERVES 4
450 g [1 lb] rock salmon
1 lemon
2.5 ml [½ teaspoon] freshly ground black pepper
5 ml [1 teaspoon] dry English mustard
2.5 ml [½ teaspoon] dried oregano
10 anchovy fillets
45 ml [3 tablespoons] olive oil
15 ml [1 tablespoon] freshly chopped parsley
45 ml [3 tablespoons] plain flour
1 large egg
90 ml [6 tablespoons] oil

1 Remove any bones from the fish and cut the flesh into lengths of 5 cm [2"].

2 Squeeze the lemon and put the juice, pepper, mustard and oregano into a bowl and mix.

3 Chop the anchovy fillets finely and add to the marinade with the olive oil and parsley. Mix well.

4 Put in the fish, stir gently for a few seconds to mix the marinade with the fish. Cover the dish loosely and leave in a cool place for at least 1–2 hours.

5 Lift the pieces of fish out of the marinade, one by one, pausing a moment to let surplus marinade drain back into the basin. Reserve the marinade.

6 Spread the flour on a sheet of greaseproof paper. Roll each piece of fish in flour to coat thoroughly and shake to remove surplus flour.

7 Beat the egg lightly in a shallow dish.

8 Pour the oil for frying into a large pan and heat gently until a cube of dry bread droppped in turns golden in about 30 seconds.

9 Dip the fish, piece by piece, in the beaten egg to coat lightly, and immediately lower into the hot fat. Do not crowd the pan. Fry for 2–3 minutes, turning once or twice, until golden and crisp all over.

10 Lift the fish out with a perforated spoon, drain briefly on crumpled kitchen paper and pile up on a hot serving dish. Keep hot and repeat with the remaining fish.

11 Immediately before serving sprinkle with a little of the marinade.

TROUT WITH ALMONDS

⊠*The charm of this popular dish depends on frying the fish in butter so that the skin of the trout is crisp and golden and the fish cooked through. The nutty flavour and texture of the almonds contrast well with trout but, portions of brill or halibut, which also seem to have a natural affinity with almonds, can be cooked in the same manner despite the lack of skin. Ask the fishmonger to clean the trout through the gills but to leave the head on. If frozen rainbow trout is used instead of fresh, it can be cooked from near frozen if fried very gently for about 15 minutes.*

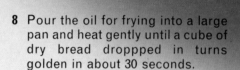

Garnish the dish with wedges or twists of lemon and watercress.

SERVES 4
4 fresh trout, each weighing about 200 g [7 oz]
60 ml [4 tablespoons] seasoned flour
75 g [3 oz] clarified butter
25 g [1 oz] butter
50 g [2 oz] flaked almonds
15 ml [1 tablespoon] lemon juice
salt
freshly ground black pepper

1 Spread the seasoned flour on a sheet of greaseproof paper and roll the fish in it, one at a time, to coat thoroughly all over. Shake off surplus flour.

2 Heat 50 g [2 oz] clarified butter in a large frying-pan and, while still foaming, put in two trout and fry gently over medium heat for 4–5 minutes until golden.

3 Turn the fish carefully and continue cooking for another 4–5

Trout with almonds is fried à la meunière as in the step-by-step instructions. Other less expensive fish, such as lemon sole, dabs, megrim and witch can also be fried this way for a simple and light meal.

minutes on the other side. Check that the fish is cooked through to the bone by making a small incision with the point of a knife in the thickest part. Lift the fish out without draining, arrange on a serving dish and keep hot.

4 Add the remaining clarified butter to the pan and cook the next two fish in the same way.

5 When all the fish are cooked, remove the pan from the heat and wipe out with kitchen paper. Put in the butter, return to the heat and, when hot, fry the almonds, stirring frequently until pale and golden brown.

6 Add the lemon juice to the pan with a light seasoning of salt and pepper. Stir, spoon over the trout and serve immediately.

BRETON-STYLE FLAT FISH

This is an attractive, quick and useful recipe for cooking flat fish such as dabs, lemon sole or megrim when they happen to be available in single portion sizes. You can ask the fishmonger to remove the heads and dark skin and trim the fins, or do this at home with a sharp knife. Use whichever fresh herbs are available, choosing from parsley, chervil and chives.

SERVES 4
4 flat fish, each weighing about 350 g [12 oz]
45 ml [3 tablespoons] seasoned flour
2 shallots
1 lemon
100 g [¼ lb] unsalted butter
30 ml [2 tablespoons] oil
50 g [2 oz] shelled shrimps
20 ml [4 teaspoons] drained capers
20 ml [4 teaspoons] chopped fresh herbs

1 Spread the seasoned flour on a sheet of greaseproof paper. Press each fish in turn into it, to coat thoroughly on both sides. Shake off surplus flour.

2 Chop the shallots finely and squeeze the lemon.

3 Heat 25 g [1 oz] butter and 15 ml [1 tablespoon] oil in a small pan. Fry the shallots gently for a minute or two until soft. Add the shrimps, capers and herbs to the pan with the lemon juice. Reduce the heat to minimum and cover the pan.

4 Heat 50 g [2 oz] butter and the remaining oil in a large, heavy-based frying-pan and, when hot, fry two of the fish gently over medium heat for 4–5 minutes. Turn carefully and brown the other side. Remove to a hot serving dish and keep hot.

5 Melt the remaining butter in the pan and repeat the frying process with the remaining two fish. Transfer to the serving dish.

6 Spoon the shrimp mixture over the fish and serve immediately.

FANCIFUL FISH CAKES

Fish cakes need never be the dreary wodges of vaguely fish-flavoured potato. They should be tasty, well-seasoned mixtures, containing at least as much fish as potato, enclosed in a crunchy golden coating. The fish and potato mixture must be cooled before being coated and fried, so the mixture can be made in advance. Although traditionally round, the cakes can be made in fish shapes, balls or ovals, and coated with cornflakes, crushed potato crisps or coarse oatmeal instead of the more usual egg and breadcrumbs. If being served to children, the cakes can be decorated with quartered slices of lemon for the gills and a slice of stuffed olive for the eyes. Serve plain for breakfast, or with a freshly made tomato sauce or a creamy smooth parsley sauce.

SERVES 4
275 g [10 oz] old potatoes
350 g [12 oz] white fish fillet
40 g [1½ oz] butter
salt
white pepper
15 ml [1 tablespoon]
   freshly chopped parsley
5 ml [1 teaspoon] lemon juice
1 small egg
2 small packets potato crisps
90 ml [6 tablespoons] oil

1 Peel the potatoes and boil in lightly salted water until tender, then drain very thoroughly. Mash in the saucepan.

2 Meanwhile, put another saucepan of water to boil and cut the fish fillet into several pieces. Use a little of the butter to grease a plate and a piece of greaseproof paper to cover the fish. Lay the fish on the buttered plate, season with salt and pepper and cover with the buttered greaseproof paper.

3 Set the plate over the saucepan of boiling water, cover with the lid and steam for 10 minutes. Drain off the liquid, remove any skin and bones and flake the fish.

4 Beat the remaining butter into the mashed potato and add the fish and the parsley. Add the lemon juice and seasoning to taste. Beat until smoothly mixed.

5 Turn on to a plate, cover loosely and leave until cold and firm.

6 Divide the cooled mixture into 6 or 8 equal portions and, on a lightly floured surface, shape the portions into ovals. Beat the egg.

7 Tip the potato crisps into a strong plastic bag and crush finely with a rolling pin. Dip fish cakes in egg.

8 Turn the crushed crisps on to a piece of greaseproof paper and coat each fish cake thoroughly. Use a palette knife to press the crumbs on and to reshape the cakes.

9 Heat the oil in a large frying-pan over medium heat. When very hot, fry a single layer of fish cakes until golden, then turn carefully and brown the other side. Lift out with a fish slice, draining briefly over the pan, then thoroughly on crumpled kitchen paper. Keep hot while frying the remaining cakes and serve immediately.

Variations

●For herring roe fish cakes, replace the white fish with 225 g [½ lb] soft herring roes, poached for 10 minutes in a little milk.
●For salmon fish cakes, replace the white fish with a 200 g [7 oz] can of pink salmon, drained and flaked.

COLD MARINATED FRIED FISH

Although the swordfish generally used for this dish in the Middle East is not often available in other countries, the dish can be made with slices of any firm fish, such as mock halibut or rock salmon, or with small, whole fresh mackerel. The fish is not coated before frying. Ask the fishmonger to slice it or buy steaks. The dish does not take long to prepare but you must allow at least an hour before serving for it to chill sufficiently.

SERVES 6
1 kg [2¼ lb] mock halibut
60 ml [4 tablespoons] olive oil
225 g [½ lb] onions
2 green peppers
2 garlic cloves
400 g [14 oz] canned tomatoes
15 ml [1 tablespoon] tomato purée
30 ml [2 tablespoons] freshly chopped parsley
salt
freshly ground black pepper
50 g [2 oz] black olives

1 Pat the fish thoroughly dry with kitchen paper.

2 Heat the oil in a large sauté pan (with a lid) over medium heat and, when hot, fry the pieces of fish fairly quickly until golden on both sides, but not cooked through. Lift out carefully and reserve.

3 Peel and thinly slice the onions; halve, de-seed and thinly slice the peppers; peel and crush the garlic.

4 Add the onion to the oil remaining in the pan, which should be about 45 ml [3 tablespoons], and fry gently for about 5 minutes until beginning to soften.

5 Add the sliced peppers and continue frying gently for a further 5 minutes.

6 Add the crushed garlic and fry for another minute.

7 Drain the canned tomatoes in a sieve over a measuring jug. Make the tomato liquid up to 150 ml [¼ pt] with water and dissolve the tomato purée in it.

8 Roughly chop the tomatoes and add to the sauté pan, with the liquid and parsley, and salt and pepper to taste. Bring to the boil and simmer for 5 minutes.

9 Lay the reserved pieces of fish gently in the pan, spooning the sauce over them if not completely covered.

10 Cover the pan and cook very gently for 10–15 minutes until the fish is cooked through.

11 Lift out the fish and arrange the pieces side by side in a shallow dish.

12 Boil the liquid rapidly, uncovered, until reduced to the consistency of a thin sauce. Add the whole black olives for the last few minutes of cooking and check the seasoning before pouring over the fish.

13 Allow to become cold and chill in the refrigerator before serving.

COD PROVENCAL-STYLE

This recipe is a useful way of adding both colour and flavour to any kind of white round fish fillets. It is particularly suitable for coley, whiting and cod, with fresh or frozen fillets. Serve with creamy mashed potatoes.

SERVES 4
700 g [1½ lb] cod fillets
30 ml [2 tablespoons] seasoned flour
1 medium-sized onion
2 garlic cloves
450 g [1 lb] tomatoes
60 ml [4 tablespoons] olive oil
5 ml [1 teaspoon] freshly chopped parsley
salt
freshly ground black pepper
25 g [1 oz] black olives

1 Skin the fillets and cut the fish roughly into 4 cm [1½"] squares.

2 Put the seasoned flour into a plastic bag. Put in the fish and toss until well coated. Remove the fish and shake off surplus flour.

3 Peel and slice the onion; peel and crush the garlic cloves; peel, de-seed and chop the tomatoes.

4 Heat 30 ml [2 tablespoons] oil in a sauté pan over low heat. When hot, put in the onion and fry gently for about 6–8 minutes until soft. Add the garlic and cook for another minute or so, then add the tomatoes, chopped parsley and salt and pepper to taste.

5 Toss over fairly brisk heat for several minutes until the tomato begins to soften, then reduce heat to minimum and cover pan.

6 Heat the remaining oil in a large frying-pan and, when sizzling hot, put in the pieces of fish. Fry over moderate heat, turning frequently, until cooked through and lightly browned on all sides. This will take about 8 minutes.

7 Remove the fish with a perforated spoon, drain on crumpled kitchen paper and transfer to a hot shallow serving dish.

8 Spoon the vegetables over the fish, garnish with whole black olives and serve immediately.

Cod Provençal-style is a tasty and colourful dish of fried fish and juicy vegetables.

MACKEREL FILLETS ANTIBOISE

▨ *Large mackerel tend to be coarse but can still make a pleasant luncheon dish if filleted, fried and served with a succulent and colourful vegetable garnish as in this recipe. For an added touch of colour, prepare some grilled tomatoes in advance as an extra garnish.*

SERVES 4
4 mackerel fillets, each weighing about 175 g [6 oz]
30 ml [2 tablespoons] seasoned flour
2 medium-sized leeks
4 young celery sticks
45 ml [3 tablespoons] olive oil
salt
freshly ground black pepper
50 g [2 oz] butter
half a lemon

1 Spread the seasoned flour on a sheet of greaseproof paper and press each mackerel fillet in turn into the flour to coat each side. Shake off surplus flour.

2 Remove the coarse outer leaves and trim the leeks. Wash them thoroughly in cold salted water, drain and then cut across into 6 mm [¼"] slices. Wash and trim the celery and cut across into 6 mm [¼"] slices.

3 Heat 30 ml [2 tablespoons] oil in a heavy-based saucepan over medium heat. Fry the leeks and celery, covered, shaking the pan frequently, for about 15 minutes or until tender. Season with salt and pepper.

4 Meanwhile, heat 25 g [1 oz] butter and the remaining oil in a large frying-pan and fry the mackerel fillets, skin side uppermost, for 4–5 minutes. Turn carefully and fry the other side for 3–4 minutes. Lift out and arrange on a hot serving dish with a space between each fillet.

5 Spoon a little of the leek and celery mixture along the space between each fillet.

6 Wipe out the pan in which the fish was cooked and put in the remaining butter. Heat briskly until it is nut brown, then immediately spoon a little over each fillet,

followed by a squeeze of lemon juice. Serve immediately.

HERRINGS FRIED IN OATMEAL

▨ *This favourite Scottish recipe is one of the best ways of cooking herrings. The crunchy overcoat of nutty-flavoured oatmeal is a perfect foil for rich and succulent fish. Splitting and boning the herrings give a larger surface area to be coated. Make sure the fish used is really fresh. Fresh, coarse oatmeal is best for coating, but if not available use rolled oats or porridge oats, lightly crisped under the grill before use. Bacon dripping makes a tasty alternative to oil for frying. Serve plain for breakfast, or with a fluffy mustard sauce for supper. Generously garnish the fish with wedges of orange and small cluster of water-cress.*

SERVES 4
4 fresh herrings, each weighing about 250-350 g [9-12 oz]
15 ml [1 tablespoon] coarse salt
freshly ground black pepper
60 ml [4 tablespoons] coarse oatmeal
90 ml [6 tablespoons] oil

1 Split and bone the herrings (see on pages 4–5) removing both head and tail

2 Rinse the fish in cold water and pat dry with kitchen paper. Sprinkle generously with salt and pepper.

3 Spread the oatmeal on a piece of greaseproof paper and press each fish in turn into the oatmeal so that it is coated on both sides.

4 Heat the oil in a large frying-pan over medium heat and, when hot, lay two of the herrings in the pan, cut side down, and fry for about 4 minutes until brown and crisp.

5 Turn the fish carefully and cook the other side for another 3–4 minutes. Watch that the fat does not get too hot or the oatmeal may burn. Reduce heat if necessary.

6 Lift out the fish and drain on kitchen paper. Place on a serving plate and keep hot while frying the remaining fish. Serve very hot.

HERRING ROE TOASTS

▨ *Soft herring roes have a rich flavour and a creamy texture. They are excellent lightly floured, fried in butter and served on toast. For this recipe you need fresh roes which will retain their shape. Roes which have been frozen in bulk are often a soft, shapeless mass when thawed and although very suitable for fish cakes or other soft mixtures, they cannot be separated into individual roes for frying. Prepare the garnish first to avoid any delay in serving.*

SERVES 2
225 g [½ lb] fresh, soft herring roes
30 ml [2 tablespoons] seasoned flour
pinch cayenne pepper
25 g [1 oz] butter
15 ml [1 tablespoon] oil

For the garnish:
2 slices of bread
15 g [½ oz] butter
half a lemon
fresh parsley

1 Toast the bread and butter it. Cut off the crusts if wished. Cut the lemon into wedges and wash the parsley and divide into small sprigs. Set aside.

2 Put the roes in a colander and wash very thoroughly with cold water. Drain well and remove any pieces of black membrane. Blot dry with kitchen paper.

3 Put the seasoned flour on a large piece of greaseproof paper, add a large pinch of cayenne pepper and mix thoroughly.

4 Put the roes, a few at a time, into the flour, lifting the corners of the paper to coat the roes completely. Lift out with tongs and shake off surplus flour.

5 Heat the butter and oil in a small frying-pan and, when hot, fry the roes, a few at a time, for about 2 minutes or until golden. Turn carefully and fry the other side until golden. Lift out and reserve while frying remaining roes.

6 Drain the roes carefully and pile on to the toast. Add a sprig of parsley and some wedges of lemon before serving.

Sea shell specials

Prawns, shrimps and scampi have always ranked among the most desirable of all seafood to eat and this course explains the difference and shows how to cook and serve these shellfish for the tastiest of meals.

Crustaceans are aquatic creatures with brittle jointed shells. These shellfish have always been sought after and, consequently, they are far from cheap. This means there is all the more reason for knowing how to choose and cook them so that, when you do buy them, they prove a real treat.

Shrimps and prawns, so delicate to look at, are in fact the scavengers of the sea shore. They feed on coastal debris and are very nutritious.

Fresh shellfish are unbeatable for flavour—whether they are the large crayfish of Australia and New Zealand, the popular Italian scampi or Dublin Bay prawn (shown on the left at the bottom of the picture below) or the tiny British common or brown shrimp.

Shrimps

This name is given to a small species, called the crevette grise in France and the gamberetto in Italy. In many countries, however, no distinction is made between prawns and shrimps.

Shrimps are found in inshore waters, and bury themselves in sand. In northern Europe there are two types: the common or brown shrimp is a grey transparent colour and goes pink when cooked. The pink shrimp is almost colourless and transparent but again turns pink when cooked. Shrimps are nearly always sold boiled.

Prawns

Prawns range in size from about 5 cm [2″] to 15 cm [6″] depending on which part of the world they come from. British prawns are greyish and partly transparent when raw, turning pink, with firm flesh, when boiled. They are usually sold ready boiled. Like shrimps they are sold in pints: one pint is equivalent to 225 g [8 oz] which after peeling will weigh 125-150 g [4-5 oz].

Prawns from Norway and Greenland are slightly larger—about

10 cm [4"] long, with a lovely melting texture. They are often imported into Britain and sold ready boiled.

The Mediterranean prawn is the largest European prawn—about 12.5 cm [5"]. It is known as crevette rose in France and gambero in Italy.

Pacific prawns are still larger, and are much darker in colour than the European prawns. They are a greenish brown colour, with a pink tinge. The flesh turns pale pink when cooked.

Frozen prawns: the larger types of prawn are often frozen for export. Pacific or king prawns are shipped frozen raw from China and Malaysia. Australian Pacific prawns are usually shipped whole if they are boiled before freezing, but have their heads removed if they are frozen raw. A dark, greenish brown freshwater prawn is exported from Bangladesh. Prawn catches from Mexico are shipped to the United States. Mediterranean prawns are also frozen and shipped all over the world.

Frozen peeled prawns can be divided into two classes. Those with the better taste and texture are caught in cold waters, in places like Canada, Greenland and Norway. Warm water prawns are caught off Malaysia, Thailand, Japan, China and Australia. They have a harder, more chewy texture, and less flavour.

Scampi

Scampi is the Italian name (scampo in the singular) for a specific type of shellfish known as the Dublin Bay prawn in Britain, but also called the Norway lobster. In France, scampi are called langoustines.

They are up to 20 cm [8"] long, although in Europe they do not usually grow to more than half this length. They have a hard, spiky, orangey pink shell with a greyish tinge, which does not change colour much when cooked. They have long pincers, but the meat is all in the tail.

They are sold ready boiled or frozen, without the head. For a main course for six people, buy 1.4 kg [3 lb] if they are in their shells, or 700 g [1½ lb] if shelled.

A selection of some of the most popular types of prawn and shrimp:
top, from the left: British prawns in their shells; shelled British prawns.
Bottom, from the left: Mediterranean prawns; the common or brown shrimp; pale pink shrimps; scampi, known as Dublin Bay prawns, Norway lobsters, or langoustines, with and without a coating of breadcrumbs; Pacific prawns, which can be identified by their dark colour, without their heads.

Crayfish

These freshwater shellfish (ecrevisses if French) are similar to scampi. They are up to 15 cm [6"] long, a greenish brown colour, with pincers like small lobsters. They are caught in the United States and in Australia, where they are very good, as well as in Europe. They are not the same as crawfish, a larger, seawater shellfish which is known as crayfish in many parts of the world.

BOILING LIVE SHELLFISH

If you do buy or catch fresh (live) scampi, prawns or shrimps, they will need to be boiled and this should be done as soon as possible. Keep them in a bucket of salted water until you are ready to cook them.

They are very quick to cook and the flavour can easily be ruined by over cooking. It is only necessary to parboil them if recooking or reheating them later.

Bring a pan of seawater to the boil, or tap water plus enough salt to make a brine strong enough for an egg to float in (about 175 g [6 oz] salt to 2.3 L [4 pt] water). Put in the shrimps, scampi or prawns and bring back to the boil. By the time it boils, the shrimps, scampi or prawns will probably be cooked, or will need only another ½–1 minute. You can test one to see if they are cooked. If it is underdone it will be soggy; over-done and it will be hard. Larger prawns will need another 4–5 minutes.

Alternatively, put prawns in a tightly covered pan and set over a high heat to cook in their own juice. Shake the pan occasionally and cook for about ten minutes or until the prawns are cooked.

SERVING FRESHLY BOILED SHELLFISH

Fresh boiled shellfish can be used for composite dishes or sauces or they can be served immediately after boiling and this, of course, shows off their fresh salty, yet sweet, taste to best advantage.

● Serve while still warm with a hollandaise-type sauce if they are large or simply with wedges of lemon if tiny shrimps.

● If only parboiled, large prawns and scampi can be placed on an oiled rack and brushed with herb-flavoured oils or herb butter and finished off under the grill.

● Wait until they are cold and serve with mayonnaise.

● To make a meal of fresh boiled prawns, serve them on a bed of crushed ice accompanied by a bowl of fresh hard-boiled eggs, some radishes or tomatoes, a bunch of watercress or lettuce hearts. Fresh brown bread, butter, a bowl of coarse salt, and a bowl of olive oil flavoured with lemon and plenty of fresh chopped herbs complete a simple but magnificent feast.

To shell or not to shell

Whether or not you shell before serving dishes such as those described above is up to you. They look prettiest in their shells and it has certain advantages. You can serve soon after cooking, and it puts some of the work into other peoples hands!

Moreover, people like to suck the juices contained in the shells as they peel them. If your guests are peeling their own prawns, it is a good idea to provide them with finger bowls.

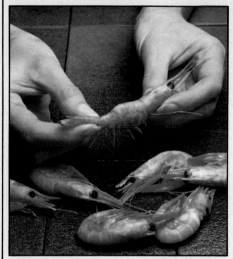  

1 Take the head in forefinger and thumb of one hand and the tail in the other and straighten out.

2 Pull the head and tail back towards each other and then gently pull them apart.

3 The tail and body shell should come off in one piece, leaving the body attached to the head.

FROZEN AND SHOP BOILED

Shellfish that is bought ready boiled, and frozen shellfish that was boiled before freezing can be used in recipes calling for fresh prawns or shrimps but the flavour is not quite as good.

Breadcrumbed and battered frozen shellfish need to be fried while frozen or the coating will come off but all other prawns and shrimps and scampi need to be thoroughly thawed. This needs to be done slowly as quick de-frosting toughens them and spoils the flavour. The liquid needs to be drained off or the dish will taste very waterlogged.

COOKING SCAMPI, PRAWNS AND SHRIMPS

The type of dish you make with these shellfish depends on two factors.

The first is whether the scampi, prawns or shrimps are fresh or frozen. As already explained, the fresher the shellfish the simpler the dish can be but frozen shellfish may need stronger accompanying flavours to mask a possible lack of taste.

The second factor is how many people you want to stretch the shellfish to feed. Obviously, rice based dishes are more economical if you want to feed several people.

The type of shellfish to be used for a dish is largely a question of individual taste and budget. Basically any shellfish can be used for any of the recipes given here. From a practical point of view, however, the larger shellfish are best in dishes where you want chunks of decorative colour, whereas tiny brown shrimps are every bit as good as larger varieties for pounded dishes such as potted shrimps, soups and sauces.

Handy hints

● The use of firm white fish is an excellent way of supplementing expensive shellfish. Dogfish and monkfish have a similar texture and go very well with shellfish. Other white fish such as coley also blend quite well with them.

● In a prawn cocktail you can use less prawns per person and substitute nuts and celery which adds a nice crunch. Try your own selection of vegetables for a different flavour.

● Make use of every bit of flavour by using fish stock, made with some prawn or shrimp shells included, as a base for sauces and soups.

COLEY AND PRAWN PIE

This is a lovely pie, using coley for economy. A good fish stock is important and both stock and wine need to be reduced to strengthen the flavour. Traditionally, savoury pies are highly decorated so use the pastry trimmings for decoration. Either make your own flaky pastry or use a bought kind. Cod is less economical.

SERVES 4
700 g [1½ lb] coley or cod fillet
100 g [¼ lb] peeled prawns
1 medium-sized onion
100 g [¼ lb] mushrooms

This pie is a deliciously creamy combination of white fish and juicy prawns served in a thick, tasty sauce.

prawns and shrimps

4 If the fish is to be used for a garnish, leave the head on the body. If not just twist and separate.

5 Check that the black vein which runs along the back is removed, some people are allergic to it.

6 Don't discard the shells as they can be saved for making fish stock for fish pies, sauces and soups.

4 sticks celery
freshly ground black pepper
salt
175 g [6 oz] flaky pastry
575 ml [1 pt] fish stock

150 ml [$\frac{1}{4}$ pt] dry white wine
60 ml [4 tablespoons] thin
  cream

50 g [2 oz] butter
30 ml [2 tablespoons] flour
1 small egg for glaze

1 Skin the coley and cut into 2.5 cm [1"] pieces. Put in a large saucepan, cover with the fish stock and poach for 5 minutes. Lift out with a slotted spoon and put into a 1.15 L [2 pt] pie or soufflé dish.

2 Strain the stock then put it in a pan with the wine and boil until it has reduced to 575 ml [1 pt].

3 Melt the butter in another pan. Peel and chop the onion and cook in the butter until softened. Finely slice the celery and add to the onion and cook for 5 minutes.

4 Wipe the mushrooms, chop the stalks and slice the caps. Add to the pan and cook for 3 minutes.

5 Stir the flour into the vegetables taking care not to break them. Remove from the heat and blend in the stock and the wine. Season.

6 Return the pan to heat and bring the sauce to the boil. Simmer for 2-3 minutes, and stir in the cream.

7 Scatter the prawns over the coley, pour over the sauce and allow to cool for 15 minutes before putting the pastry over the top.

8 Meanwhile heat the oven to 200°C [400°F] gas mark 6.

9 Roll out the pastry 6 mm [¼"] thick, large enough to overlap the pie dish. Roll the remainder thinner and cut 2 strips, each 12 mm [½"] wide.

10 Cover the prepared pie, seal edges and decorate with the trimmings. Brush with beaten egg and cook for 20-30 minutes until well risen and golden brown.

PRAWNS CREOLE

This is a lovely main course dish served with boiled long grain rice. Shrimps can be used instead of prawns and frozen ones can be used. They need to be well drained before adding to the sauce.

SERVES 4
**225 g [8 oz] peeled prawns
1 small onion
1 small green pepper
25 g [1 oz] butter
30-45 ml [2-3 tablespoons] flour**

**650 g [1 lb 7 oz] canned tomatoes
5 ml [1 teaspoon] each of rosemary, thyme and oregano
salt and pepper
5-10 ml [1-2 teaspoons] sugar**

1 Skin and finely chop onion, deseed and chop pepper and fry both in the butter for 5-10 minutes until soft.

2 Stir in the flour and gradually add the tomatoes, roughly chopped, and the herbs, salt, pepper and sugar.

3 Simmer gently for about 15 minutes until the sauce thickens and the flavours are blended.

4 Add the prawns and cook for a further 5 minutes to heat them through. Serve with the boiled rice.

PRAWNS EN COCOTTE

This is a delicately flavoured dish which can be served in small individual ramekin dishes or scallop shells. (For fish stock see the recipes on pages 44–45.) If you are not making this dish in advance it can be finished by browning the breadcrumbs under the grill instead of reheating and browning in the oven.

SERVES 4
**175 g [6 oz] large peeled prawns
1 small bulb fennel
150 ml [¼ pt] milk, infused for 15 minutes with 5 ml [1 teaspoon] fennel seeds
150 ml [¼ pt] fish stock
225 ml [8 fl oz] dry white wine
1 shallot, chopped or 1 slice of onion
1 blade mace
1 small bay leaf
6 black peppercorns
45 ml [3 tablespoons] thin cream
25–30 g [1–1¼ oz] butter
25 g [1 oz] flour
salt and pepper
fresh white breadcrumbs
a little extra butter**

1 In a small saucepan boil the wine with the chopped shallot or onion and the blade of mace, bay leaf and peppercorns, until it is reduced to

150 ml [¼ pt]. Strain the wine.

2 Wash fennel and slice into 12 mm [½"] thick strips. Poach for 5 minutes in the strained, infused milk. Strain and set aside milk and fennel.

3 Add 15 ml [1 tablespoon] of the fennel to each ramekin dish. Divide the prawns between the dishes.

4 To make a velouté sauce, melt the butter in a saucepan. Remove from heat and stir in the flour.

5 Return to the heat and cook gently without stirring until it is pale straw colour. Remove from the heat and blend in the fish stock and strained wine.

6 Slowly bring to the boil, add the milk and simmer for 2–3 minutes. Add the cream and season with salt and pepper.

7 Pour the sauce over the prawns and fennel. This can all be done in advance.

8 Heat the oven to 200°C [400°F] gas mark 6.

9 To finish, cover the top of the ramekin dishes with the breadcrumbs, dot with the extra butter and bake for 15 minutes or until the top is golden.

PRAWN NEWBURG

This delicious dish can also be made with lobster or shrimps. It can be served with either boiled rice or hot buttered toast.

SERVES 4
**225 g [8 oz] peeled prawns
25 g [1 oz] butter
60 ml [4 tablespoons] Madeira or sherry
2 large egg yolks
425 ml [¾ pt] thin cream
salt
cayenne pepper
chopped chives or parsley to garnish**

1 Sauté the prawns (reserving a few for garnishing) very gently in the butter for about 5 minutes. Stir in the Madeira or sherry and cook for another 2–3 minutes.

2 Mix the cream and egg yolks and pour into the prawn mixture. Add seasonings to taste.

3 Heat very gently until a thickened creamy consistency is obtained. Serve poured over boiled rice or with toast.

4 Sprinkle with chives or parsley and garnish with the reserved prawns.

POTTED SHRIMPS

⊠⊠ *This recipe makes a lovely first course served on its own with brown bread or on Melba toast.*

SERVES 4
450 g [1 lb] shelled shrimps
100 g [4 oz] butter
2.5 ml [½ teaspoon] ground mace
a pinch of cayenne pepper
2.5 ml [½ teaspoon] ground nutmeg
clarified butter

1 Melt the butter in a pan and add the shrimps. Heat them up slowly but do not let them boil.

2 Add the seasonings and then pour the shrimps into small pots or glasses.

Potted shrimps are sealed in clarified butter, so can be kept for a few days. They look attractive in individual ramekins, in small jars or in chunky tumblers.

3 Leave them to become quite cold and then cover each pot with a little clarified butter. Use within a few days.

4 Leave in the pots if they are really attractive, otherwise turn them out and serve on individual plates lined with a few lettuce leaves, trying to retain the shape of the pot.

PRAWN PASTE

The combination or prawn and basil makes a delightful, delicately flavoured paste. It can be made in a hurry, if necessary, by putting all the ingredients in a liquidizer and blending at top speed.

SERVES 3–4

225 g [½ lb] cooked, peeled prawns
20–30 ml [4–6 teaspoons] olive oil
2.5 ml [½ teaspoon] finely chopped basil
pinch of cayenne pepper
juice of 1 lime or half a lemon
1.5 ml [¼ teaspoon] crushed coriander or cumin seed (optional)

1 Pound or mash the prawns to a paste and very gradually add the olive oil.

2 Season with the cayenne pepper and finely chopped basil. Add the strained lemon or lime juice.

3 When the mixture is smooth, add the coriander or cumin and check the seasoning—salt may or may not be necessary depending how much has been cooked with the prawns.

4 Pack the paste in a little jar or terrine. Cover and store in the refrigerator (but not for more than 2 days). Serve chilled with toast.

SCAMPI ON SKEWERS

This is a delicious dish of Italian origin. The scampi are coated with egg and breadcrumbs and put on skewers, fried in butter and then served with lemon wedges. It can be used as a starter or as a main course on a bed of plain boiled rice with a side salad.

SERVES 4

8 pieces of scampi
8 rashers of bacon
225 g [½ lb] button mushrooms
60 ml [4 tablespoons] white breadcrumbs
15 ml [3 teaspoons] chopped sage
zest of 1 large lemon
1 large egg, beaten with a pinch of salt
30 ml [2 tablespoons] seasoned flour
50 g [2 oz] butter

1 Dry the scampi (if thawed). Wipe the mushrooms. Put the seasoned flour and beaten egg on two separate plates.

2 Mix the breadcrumbs with two thirds of the sage and the lemon zest and put on another plate.

3 Coat the scampi with flour, egg and breadcrumbs, pressing the flavoured crumbs on firmly.

4 Melt the butter in a medium-sized frying-pan—there should be enough to cover the bottom of the pan, and add the rest of the sage.

5 Thread the scampi lengthways on the skewers. Roll the rashers of bacon and thread these and the mushrooms alternately.

6 When the butter is foaming put the skewers into the pan and fry over a moderate heat for 6-8 minutes, turning 4-5 times until golden brown all over. Serve immediately.

Variation

●Scampi kebabs with cream is a nice dish. Use 1 kg [2¼ lb] of mixed monkfish, scampi, blanched baby onions and wedges of red pepper on skewers. Season and brush with melted butter. Pour 30 ml [2 tablespoons] sherry and about 150 ml [¼ pt] water into the bottom of a gratin dish. Place the kebabs in this and grill, basting while they cook. Keep the fish hot and strain the liquid into a pan and allow to bubble up and reduce until syrupy. Add 125 ml [4 fl oz] fresh thin or sour cream mixed with 15 ml [1 tablespoon] French mustard and cook until hot and reduced a little. Serve with the kebabs.

SCAMPI FILLETS

This makes a delicious luxury dish which actually isn't very expensive.

SERVES 4

8 fillets of John Dory or other flat fish
8 peeled scampi
30 ml [2 tablespoons] seasoned flour
50 g [2 oz] melted butter
125 ml [4 fl oz] white wine or cider
chopped parsley

1 large egg, hardboiled
5 ml [1 teaspoon] sage

1 Plunge the fillets of John Dory into hot water. Drain and dry well and sprinkle with seasoned flour.

2 Roll each fillet round a peeled scampi and secure with a toothpick. Put into a buttered gratin dish and brush with the melted butter and sage.

3 Cook uncovered at 180°C [350°F] gas mark 4 for 20 minutes. Gradually add the wine or cider during this time by adding and basting every 5 minutes.

4 Cover with buttered paper and cook for a further 10 minutes. Garnish with chopped parsley and sieved hard-boiled egg yolk and chopped white of egg.

ICED SHRIMP SOUP

This delicately flavoured iced soup is a delicious first course for a summertime dinner party.

SERVES 4

225 g [½ lb] boiled shrimps
350 g [¾ lb] white fish fillet
1 small lemon, and juice of half a lemon
2 large tomatoes
1 small onion
5 ml [1 teaspoon] dried dill
45 ml [3 tablespoons] white breadcrumbs
pinch of nutmeg
15 ml [1 tablespoon] thick cream
cucumber for garnish

1 Peel the shrimps and place the shells in a pan with the white fish, complete with skin.

2 Slice the lemon, tomatoes, and onion and add to the pan with the dill and 850 ml [1½ pt] water. Simmer for 20 minutes and then strain.

3 Put the shrimps (except for a few for garnishing) in a blender with the breadcrumbs, the juice of half a lemon and the nutmeg. Add the strained stock and liquidize.

4 Chill and then blend in a swirl of cream and garnish with paper thin slices of cucumber and a few whole shrimps.

The king of the river

To cooks, gourmets and fishermen alike, the salmon is the king of the river. Handsome to serve and delicious to eat, this elegant, pink fish will turn any meal into a very special occasion. The salmon is both elusive and expensive in its finest form but cheaper alternatives are available, such as frozen Pacific salmon, grilse and salmon trout.

The salmon is a migratory fish, dividing its time between river and sea. It spawns in the gravel beds in the upper reaches of the salmon rivers and there the tiny salmon or 'fingerling' stay and develop for two or three years. Then, as 'smolts', they swim in a shoal down the river and far out to sea. At sea they feed and develop for one, two or even three years until they are ready to return to the river to spawn. Miraculously, the salmon invariably return to the river in which they were born and swim upstream against endless hazards until the survivors reach the spawning grounds and the life cycle begins again.

The salmon 'run', or swim up the river, either in the early months of the year, when they are known as spring or first run fish, or later in summer when they are called summer or second run fish. Fresh, first run fish are the finest, with a particularly delicate flavour and command a correspondingly high price. As the season when fishing is allowed progresses and supplies increase the price usually falls.

TYPES OF FISH
Fresh salmon is very delicious but also very expensive. It can be bought frozen but the flavour cannot be

compared to that of fresh salmon. Grilse and salmon are cheaper but equally delicious alternatives.

Atlantic salmon

This is the species fished in countries bordering the north Atlantic ocean. Those caught in the rivers of Scotland, Ireland, Wales, England and Norway are especially esteemed for their quality and fine flavour. If you buy fresh salmon in Britain it will certainly be Atlantic salmon.

The body of the salmon is plump and the head small in comparison with Pacific salmon. The fish has a forked tail and its shining skin varies from steely grey on the back, through silver to a white belly. Black spots appear above the lateral line. The weight of a whole fresh salmon can vary from 3-9.1 kg [7-20 lb].

In Britain, the season lasts roughly from February to the end of the summer, exact dates varying a little between Scotland, England and Ireland. The peak season for fresh salmon, when supplies are at their greatest, is June to July. Early season fresh Atlantic salmon is best prepared by very simple methods so that the delicate flavour is not lost.

Pacific salmon

The salmon which proliferate in the Pacific ocean are fished in American, Canadian and Russian rivers and are eaten fresh in these countries. There are five different species of Pacific salmon and several of them are exported canned or frozen.

Frozen Pacific salmon is available exported all the year round and is usually considerably cheaper than fresh salmon. It is gutted and beheaded before freezing and, although similar to the Atlantic salmon, its body is flatter and the skin duller once it has thawed. The average weight of the fish is 2.2-3.6 kg [5-8 lb].

Frozen salmon, although by no means as fine as fresh salmon, is excellent served with well-flavoured sauces or made into dishes such as mousse or kedgeree.

Grilse

This is the name given to a young salmon returning to its native river to spawn for the first time. It is sold fresh or frozen and is available during the early summer. It looks the same as fresh salmon, except that it is, of course, smaller. The average weight of a grilse is between 1.4-3.6 kg [3-8 lb]. Grilse is ideal for a small dinner party and can be served in any of the ways suitable for salmon.

Salmon trout

This fish is also known as sea trout, sewin and peal as well as by many other local names. Many people consider this to be the best of all river fish, combining as it does the finest qualities of salmon and trout.

Its silvery skin, streamlined shape and pink flesh resemble a grilse or young salmon, but it is, in fact, a migratory member of the brown trout family. Its head is blunter and the tail not so forked as that of a salmon. The fish usually has dark spots below as well as above the lateral line and weighs between 1-1.8 kg [2¼-4 lb], although they can reach 4.5 kg [10 lb].

Fresh Atlantic salmon (top) is identified by its size and by its being whole. Grilse (middle right) is smaller but similar in appearance, while salmon trout (middle left) is smaller still. Frozen salmon (bottom right) is always headless. Salmon cuts reveal the pink flesh.

The fish can be cooked and served in the same way as salmon but being small is particularly good cooked whole.

BUYING THE FISH

Always buy salmon and salmon trout from a high quality fishmonger. When you are buying expensive fish you want to be certain that you are also buying quality.

Fresh whole fish: a fresh salmon or salmon trout is stiff and firm with a sparkling silvery glint to its skin. The eyes should be full and bright and the gills bright red. Be wary of dull, flabby fish with sunken eyes. A fish that is headless will probably have been imported and, therefore, have been frozen.

Salmon is a substantial and firm-fleshed fish and portions do not need to be large. Apart from the central bone, there are few bones to worry about, but if buying a whole, fresh fish, remember to allow for the head and tail wastage. Consider also the size of your pan and preferably buy a fish that will fit in whole. If need be, it can be cut in half. If the fish weighs less than 1.5 kg [3½ lb] including the head and tail, allow 200-225 g [7-8 oz] per portion. If it weighs more than 1.6 kg [3½ lb], allow 150 g [5 oz] per portion.

Ask the fishmonger to leave the head and tail on but to remove the gills and eyes and gut the fish. If the fish is to be served whole, it need not be scaled or the fins trimmed unless it is to be served in its skin. If you prefer to prepare the fish yourself, instructions for all these processes are given on pages 4–5.

Cuts and steaks: ask to see the whole fish and then have taken from it the cut that you want. If this is not possible, look carefully at the skin on the individual portions to make sure it is bright and silvery and that the flesh is firm, pale pink and freshly cut. Cutlets are taken from the head end, where the fish has been gutted, and steaks from below the belly, down to the tail. Steaks cut from the tail piece will be cheaper but this part of the fish does contain more bone and you will need to allow a greater weight per portion. For middle cut steaks and cutlets allow 150-175 g [5-6 oz] per portion and for tail piece steaks, 200 g [7 oz]. The slices will be about 2-2.5 cm [¾-1"] thick from a medium-sized fish. If the fish is particularly large

and one slice too much for one portion, it can be divided in half after cooking.

When buying steaks and cutlets it is sensible, whenever possible, to have as large a surface area of skin as possible. This acts as a natural waterproof barrier, helps to keep the fish moist and protects it while it cooks. The fish can be sliced into portions after cooking.

STORING THE FISH

Ideally, salmon should be cooked as soon as possible after it has been caught, when it is at its most succulent and the cooked flesh has traces of a creamy curd-like substance between the flakes. This is unlikely to be possible unless you live in the immediate vicinity of the salmon rivers. All fish should preferably be cooked on the day it is bought and should never be kept uncooked for longer than 24 hours.

Clean the fish, if not already done by the fishmonger, and wipe it with a clean, damp cloth. Scrape the belly cavity and remove any congealed blood. Season the cavity generously with salt and pepper and keep covered and refrigerated until needed.

Salmon can be packaged and quick frozen for longer storage, whole or in portions. A whole fish should be very thoroughly scaled and cleaned and can be left complete, head and tail intact. Small or medium-sized salmon are better suited to freezing than large fish and can be kept safely for two months.

Cooked fish can be stored loosely wrapped in foil or cling film in the refrigerator for a few days; some people prefer it when the creamy curds have disappeared and the flesh is firmer.

COOKING SALMON
Fresh salmon

Although our 19th century forbears suffered from a surfeit of salmon, at today's prices our problem is not finding new ways of serving it, but cooking the occasional fish that comes our way with infinite care to conserve every scrap of its fine flavour and succulence.

The one cardinal rule is never to overcook salmon. Although it is an oily fish, overcooking makes the flesh dry and dense and it can become quite chewy in texture. Cooking

should always be gentle and cuts or slices must be wrapped loosely in foil so that all the juices are retained.

Spring salmon caught in the first weeks of the season is so delicate and delicious that it should be cooked in the simplest possible manner. The traditional Scottish method is to poach whole salmon lightly in salted water. A whole fish can also be poached in a simple court-bouillon. Two methods are described here: One where the fish can be served hot or cold, and one specially designed for serving the fish cold.

Baking is the alternative to poaching a whole fish: the fish is wrapped in foil and baked in the oven (see pages 34–35). A comprehensive section on poaching fish can be found on pages 41–51 and baking fish on pages 32–40. The methods are the same for poaching or baking salmon but because the fish is very large, the timing varies slightly. Times for poaching and baking salmon are given in the chart and, for poaching, are taken from the moment the liquid reaches simmering point.

Cuts and slices of salmon, having been wrapped loosely in foil with the ends secured (so that cut surfaces do not come into contact with water) can be poached or baked. Unwrapped slices can also be grilled, steamed or shallow fried, and these processes are described in great detail on pages 11–20, 21–31 and 79–85 respectively.

Sauces for early season salmon are best confined to melted butter for hot salmon and mayonnaise for cold salmon. Later in the season, as the fish become more plentiful, the flesh firmer and the flavour less delicate, both cooking methods and added flavours can be more robust.

Frozen salmon

To avoid the risk of overcooking, it is best to completely thaw whole salmon or large cuts so there is no danger of the outside becoming overcooked before the centre is cooked through. Ideally, leave the salmon in its packaging in a refrigerator, allowing about 18 hours for a 1-1.8 kg [2¼-4 lb] piece to thaw and from 24-36 hours for a whole medium-sized fish. For speedier thawing at room temperature, allow roughly 3-4 hours per 450 g [1 lb].

Steaks or cutlets are thin enough for the heat to penetrate fairly quickly, so these can be cooked from frozen, allowing about half as long again as when cooking fresh or fully thawed fish.

Equipment for poaching

The average salmon is a fairly large fish and may cause some problems in the kitchen finding a pan large enough to take the fish whole. If you cook whole salmon or other large fish fairly frequently, a fish kettle is a useful piece of equipment. This is a long, deep pan fitted with a perforated plate with long handles. The fish lies on the plate, just above the base of the pan, so that the liquid just covers it. The perforated plate makes lifting the fish in and out easy and there is no danger of burning or scalding yourself.

There are various ways in which a fish kettle can be improvised and these are detailed on pages 42–43. You will, however, still need a pan that is long enough to take the length of the fish. The alternative to this, if you have no such pan, is to cut the fish in half and wrap the cut surfaces securely in foil. This will prevent any of the natural juices seeping into the water. The two pieces can then be cooked side by side.

Fish poached in this way can be served hot or cold. There is an alternative method for poaching salmon that is to be served cold which is designed to keep the fish moist while it cools.

No-cook poaching method for salmon to be served cold

This method avoids any possibility of overcooking the fish, by giving it a very brief simmering time. It is then allowed to cool slowly in the liquid so that the flesh remains beautifully moist and succulent.

A whole fish or any size cut of fish can be cooked by this method, provided you have a fish kettle or pan large enough and deep enough to contain the fish plus enough water to cover it completely with 2.5 cm [1"] to spare. The larger the fish the more water will be required and the longer it will take to cool, thus the method adapts itself to any size of salmon or salmon cut.

COOKING TIMES FOR FRESH SALMON		
Weight	Poaching	Baking
1.4 kg [3 lb]	25–30 minutes	45 minutes
2.2 kg [5 lb]	40–50 minutes	65-68 minutes
3.2 kg [7 lb]	50–60 minutes	80 minutes
3.6 kg [8 lb]	55–65 minutes	88-90 minutes
4.5 kg [10 lb]	60–75 minutes	95 minutes
5.4 kg [12 lb]	65–80 minutes	100 minutes
6.8 kg [15 lb]	75–90 minutes	110 minutes
8.2 kg [18 lb]	85–100 minutes	118 minutes
9.1 kg [20 lb]	95–105 minutes	125 minutes

You must allow time for complete cooling which, in the case of a whole salmon, will be overnight. Cuts of fish should be wrapped in foil to prevent any juices escaping into the water. The juices are retained in the foil and can be used for flavouring sauces.

If cooking a piece of fish, cut a piece of foil large enough to enclose the fish generously and brush it with oil. You must use oil, not melted butter, as this would solidify as it cooled. Place the prepared fish in the foil, wrap it loosely and twist the edges together tightly to make a loose but completely waterproof parcel.

Place the parcel, or the unwrapped whole fish, in your chosen cooking vessel and add enough cold water to cover the fish by 2.5 cm [1"]. Bring the water to the boil, reduce the heat to maintain a simmer and simmer the fish for 5 minutes. Do not cook fish for longer.

Remove the pan from the heat, cover it tightly and transfer it to a cool place where it can stand undisturbed. Leave the pan until the water is cool but not absolutely cold as it is much easier to remove the skin from the fish while it is still faintly warm. The skinned fish can be stored, loosely covered, in the refrigerator until it is needed.

SKINNING AND BONING COOKED SALMON

The distinctive colour of the flesh of a salmon is part of its attraction. It can vary from a very delicate pale pink to a much deeper shade, verging on red. It is a shame not to present the fish to its best advantage and the time needed to skin the fish is well worth it.

Salmon to be served hot can be left in its skin, provided the fish has been scaled and the fins trimmed, or can be served with the upper surface revealed. If the fish has been cooked unscaled or is to be served cold, it should be completely skinned.

Whole fish

If these are large they will require careful handling, but the method is the same for any size fish. Lay the fish on a piece of damp greaseproof paper on a flat surface. Use a sharp knife and cut through the skin across the tail, around the head and down the length of the backbone. Peel off the skin with the knife, taking any fins with it, until the upper surface is revealed. Gently scrape away the shallow layer of brown-coloured flesh that usually runs along the centre of the fish and reserve this for a made-up dish. With the help of the greaseproof paper, roll the fish over and repeat the operation on the other side.

Boning is not essential, but it does make the portioning and serving of the fish easier. First, loosen the upper fillet by inserting a knife between it and the bone. Lift off the fillet and reserve. In the case of a large fish, it may be easier to divide the fillet along the middle and lift it off in two pieces. Snip through the bone at the head and tail and peel it off from one end. Carefully replace the upper fillet. Move the fish very carefully to a serving dish, either with fish slice or by sliding it off the greaseproof paper. If the fish breaks during this process the 'joins' can easily be concealed by a garnish.

Steaks and cutlets

These are very simple to skin. Ease a knife around the fish and peel away the skin gently. Loosen the central bone and lift out.

SERVING SALMON

The choice of accompaniments depends entirely on the quality of the salmon being served. If you are

Step-by-step to skinning and boning

1 Take the fish and lay it on a large sheet of damp greaseproof paper on a flat surface.

2 Take a sharp knife and cut the skin across the tail, round the head and along the top of the fish.

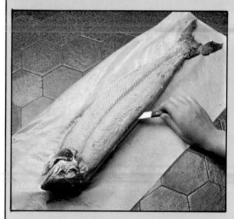

6 Pass the knife in under the upper fillet, flat against the bone, and work it along the fish.

7 Lift off the upper fillet very carefully, using two fish slices, and lay it on greaseproof paper.

fortunate to have some fresh spring salmon, or later in the season some grilse or salmon trout, you will not want to overpower their delicate flavour with heavy sauces and robust vegetable dishes; reserve these for late season or imported frozen fish.

Sauces and butters

The ideal accompaniment for prime quality salmon served hot is plain melted butter and served cold, a light, lemon-flavoured, home-made mayonnaise. Later in the season the melted butter can be replaced by any of the following sauces: hollandaise, béarnaise or mousseline. Home-made mayonnaise can be flavoured with several variations such as chantilly, rémoulade, mayonnaise verte, gribiche and tartare. If using bought mayonnaise, use an egg-based one.

When serving cold salmon there are two alternatives to providing a separate sauce. The fish can be

coated with aspic or a chaudfroid sauce. These make the presentation particularly handsome and are recommended for a special occasion. Making aspic and chaudfroid is a very involved process so allow yourself plenty of time.

Vegetables

Vegetables should be kept very simple so as not to detract from the fish and only a limited number should be served. The obvious accompaniment to cold salmon is a crisp, green salad with a light dressing and some potatoes, either new, boiled and tossed in butter or a potato salad. New potatoes, boiled in their skins and tossed in butter are ideal with hot salmon and can be lightly flavoured with chopped parsley, dill, chives or tarragon. Sautéed vegetables, such as cucumber, courgettes and mushrooms, young spinach, asparagus and French beans are all suitable.

a whole salmon

3 Peel the skin away from one end, using the knife to prize it away from the flesh.

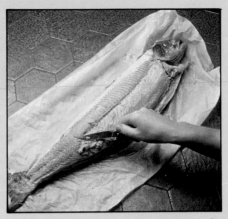

4 Discard the skin and with the knife, scrape away the brown flesh from the middle of the fish.

5 Using the greaseproof paper, roll the fish over and repeat the skinning process on the underside.

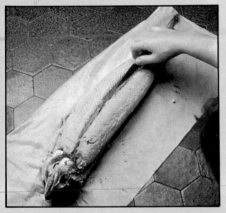

OR run a knife along the length of the fish to divide the upper fillet in two. Lift off each half.

8 Snip through the backbone at the tail and the head and peel it away from the lower fillet.

9 Lift the upper fillet back into position. Transfer the whole fish to a serving dish and garnish.

POACHED SALMON

If you are poaching a large fish, a fish kettle will be very useful. If you have not got one, try one of the improvisations given on pages 42–43. A recipe for the court-bouillon appears on page 44; it must be cool when it is used. Choose your accompaniments according to the season but be careful not to detract from the delicate flavour of the fish. The suggestion given here is for a sauce called a mousseline which is a creamier version of a hollandaise sauce, excellent served with fine-flavoured salmon. The fish can, of course, be served cold with a mayonnaise.

SERVES 15–18
1 fresh salmon, weighing 2.7 kg [6 lb]
salt and pepper
1.7 L [3 pts] general-purpose court-bouillon
575 ml [1 pt] sauce mousseline

1 Wipe the salmon with a clean damp cloth, remove any congealed blood from around the belly cavity and season with salt and pepper.

2 Place the fish on the perforated plate and, using the long handles, lower the plate into the kettle. Pour in sufficient cool court-bouillon to barely cover the fish.

3 Put the lid on the pan and bring the liquid to simmering point on a low heat. Adjust the heat to keep the bouillon at just below simmering point: it should quiver but not bubble.

4 Poach the fish for the calculated time, taken from the moment the water reaches simmering point. Test with a thin skewer to see if it is cooked.

5 Raise the perforated plate out of

the pan and lay it across the kettle to drain for 5 minutes.

6 Carefully remove the fish to a warm serving dish. Skin the upper surface if desired and garnish as wished.

Variation

● To serve the fish cold, after draining transfer the fish to a shallow dish or pan and leave undisturbed in a cool place. When cool, skin the fish and if you have not got a large enough serving dish put the fish on a foil-covered board with the head and tail on some sprigs of watercress. Use slices of cucumber to garnish the fish and arrange slices of lemon against the sides of the fish.

When salmon is cold it can be garnished in a variety of ways. Bearing in mind that the flesh is pink, try to include some greenery and colourful tomatoes.

SALMON TROUT BAKED IN FOIL

This is one of the best methods of cooking fresh salmon trout. The method can also be used for grilse, salmon cuts and whole small and medium-sized salmon and, is very useful when you do not have a pan large enough to use for poaching. A large fish can be cut in half and wrapped in two separate parcels, the timing being calculated on the weight of each parcel rather than the total weight. A medium-sized fish may need to be 'persuaded' to fit into the oven by curving it on its stomach. The head and tail may touch the sides of the oven but will be protected by the foil. Fish cooked in this way can be eaten hot or cold.

The hollandaise sauce is the perfect accompaniment to baked trout. Serve with new potatoes, tossed in butter and chopped parsley.

If you wish to serve the fish cold, grease the foil with oil rather than butter and when baked, remove the parcel to a cool place and leave the fish until cool but not cold, before skinning and refrigerating until needed.

SERVES 6
1 salmon trout weighing 1.4 kg [3 lb]

salt and pepper
15 ml [1 tablespoon] melted butter
425 ml [¾ pt] hollandaise sauce
fresh dill for garnish

1 Heat the oven to 180°C [350°F] gas mark 4. Put a baking tray on the centre shelf.

2 Make sure the belly cavity of the fish is quite clean and season it well with salt and pepper if you have not already done so.

3 Weigh the fish and calculate the cooking time.

4 Cut a large piece of foil in which to wrap the fish and grease this generously with melted butter.

5 Lay the fish in the middle of the foil. Fold the foil over and twist the edges together firmly. The parcel must be loose but secure.

6 Place the parcel on the hot baking tray or, if the fish is large and has to be curled slightly, directly on the oven shelf.

7 Bake for 45 minutes and remove from the oven.

8 Leave the fish to rest in the unopened foil for 10 minutes. Transfer the whole parcel to a warm serving dish and carefully fold back the foil. With a sharp knife, skin the upper surface of the fish and garnish with the fresh dill.

KOULIBIAC

This is a traditional Russian recipe, originally made with a yeast pastry but nowadays usually with puff or flaky pastry. Although some recipes suggest using leftover cooked salmon it is much better made with freshly cooked salmon. The recipe is a very rich one, so the traditional custom of pouring melted butter into the vent holes just before serving has been omitted. If you want to do this, use 25 g [1 oz] extra butter. Season the filling really well, adding the lemon juice to offset the richness. The chicken stock may be made with a cube. The cold cucumber sauce is a good lubricant and contrast.

Baking in foil is particularly recommended for fresh salmon trout to preserve its delicate flavour. It makes a lovely party dish, hot or cold. Koulibiac is a delicious pie made with puff pastry.

SERVES 8–10

450 g [1 lb] middle cut salmon
100 g [¼ lb] long grain rice
275 ml [½ pt] cold chicken
    stock
salt
freshly ground black pepper
75 g [3 oz] butter
100 g [¼ lb] mild onion or
    shallots
100 g [¼ lb] small button
    mushrooms
30 ml [2 tablespoons] freshly
    chopped parsley
juice of a lemon
pinch of grated nutmeg
400 g [14 oz] puff pastry
2 hard-boiled eggs
1 egg beaten

To serve:
sour cream and cucumber
    sauce

1 Put the rice, stock and 1.25 ml [¼ teaspoon] salt into a saucepan and bring to the boil. Stir, cover tightly and simmer for 15-20 minutes until all the stock has been absorbed and the rice is dry and fluffy.

2 Cut the salmon into 6 mm [¼"] slices and season them with salt and pepper.

3 Melt 50 g [2 oz] butter in a large frying pan and lightly fry the slices of fish for 2-3 minutes each side. Lift out and leave to cool.

4 Meanwhile peel and finely chop the onion or shallots.

5 Add the remaining butter to the frying pan, put in the onion and fry gently for about 10 minutes until soft and golden.

6 Meanwhile wipe and finely slice the mushrooms.

7 Add the mushrooms to the onions, stir well and continue frying gently for another 4-5 minutes.

8 Meanwhile remove the skin and flake the fish coarsely, carefully removing all bones as you do so.

9 Add the cooked rice, flaked fish and chopped parsley to the onion and mushroom mixture and season with lemon juice, nutmeg and salt and pepper to taste. Mix well and set aside to cool.

10 Heat the oven to 200°C [400°F] gas mark 6.

11 Divide the pastry in half and roll out each piece into an oblong measuring 30 × 23 cm [12 × 9"]. Cut a 2.5 cm [1"] strip off the shorter side of each piece and reserve.

12 Lay one oblong of pastry on a flat baking sheet. Cover it with the cold rice and fish mixture, leaving a 1.25 cm [½"] margin around the edges.

13 Slice the hard boiled eggs thinly and lay over the mixture.

14 Dampen the edges of the pastry with water, lay the second oblong

of pastry on top and press the edges together to seal them. Seal the edges with the back of a knife.

15 Make two vent holes in the centre of the top layer of pastry for the steam to escape. Cut the reserved strips of pastry into leaves and use to decorate around the holes

16 Brush pastry with beaten egg.

17 Bake towards the top of the oven for about 30-40 minutes, until the pastry is cooked and golden.

18 Serve hot, with cold cucumber sauce handed separately.

SALMON TROUT EN GELEE

This is a lovely dish for summer supper parties and very simple to prepare. Cook the fish in the morning so that it is cold and ready to decorate in the afternoon. If you haven't a dish long enough on which to serve it, use a clean plank of wood covered with foil instead, and adjust the garnish accordingly. For mayonnaise chantilly season 425 ml [¾ pt] with the juice of half a lemon and then fold in 40 ml [3 tablespoons] whipped cream.

SERVES 6
1 salmon trout weighing 1.4 kg [3 lb]
salt
freshly ground black pepper
oil
575 ml [1 pt] aspic jelly

For the garnish:
1 cucumber, thinly sliced
1 sprig fresh tarragon or fennel
2 hard-boiled eggs, quartered lengthways

To serve:
425 ml [¾ pt] mayonnaise Chantilly

Two very different dishes which both make tasty meals. Serve salmon kedgeree as a change from the usual smoked fish version and salmon trout when you want to impress. Left-over salmon may be used for the salmon kedgeree, but the salmon trout dish requires fresh fish.

1 Heat the oven to 180°C [350°F] gas mark 4 and put a baking tray on the centre shelf.

2 Wipe·the fish with a clean damp cloth, scrape the body cavity and season it with salt and freshly ground black pepper.

3 Cut a piece of foil 15 cm [6"] longer than the fish and brush it liberally with oil.

4 Lay the fish on the foil and twist the foil edges together to make a loose but watertight parcel.

5 Place on the baking tray and bake in the centre of the oven for 45 minutes.

6 When the fish is cooked remove the parcel from the oven and leave in a cold place, unopened, until cool.

7 Open the parcel and skin the fish before it becomes cold, following the directions for skinning given in the step-by-step instructions.

8 Carefully lift the fish, supporting the head and tail as you do so, and lay flat on a serving dish.

9 Check that the aspic jelly is cold and almost setting (if not, stand it over crushed ice and stir until it coats the back of the spoon), then spoon a thin film of jelly over the fish. Leave to set.

10 Arrange a very simple garnish on the fish such as a spray of tarragon leaves or a frond of fennel. Set the garnish by glazing with another layer of jelly.

12 Leave in a cold place to set, and chill the remaining aspic.

13 To serve, chop the aspic jelly on a piece of wet greaseproof paper and arrange along either side of the fish. Border the dish with overlapping slices of crimped cucumber and arrange the pieces of egg on either side. Just before serving, tuck a few small fronds of fennel into any gaps. Hand round the mayonnaise Chantilly separately.

SALMON KEDGEREE

A kedgeree of salmon is one of the prettiest of dishes, as well as an excellent way of making a small amount of cooked salmon into a rather special supper or buffet party dish. Use left-over or freshly cooked salmon. This recipe uses a fairly high proportion of fish to rice, so if an extra guest turns up unexpectedly you need have no fear about adding an extra 50 g [2 oz] rice. The quantity of butter ensures a creamy tasting kegeree, but if you like a soft creamy texture add the optional cream.

SERVES 4-6
225 g [½ lb] long grain rice
5 ml [1 teaspoon] salt
1 medium-sized onion
100 g [¼ lb] butter,
 preferably unsalted
450 g [1 lb] cooked salmon
1 hard-boiled egg
30 ml [2 tablespoons] chopped
 chives (optional)
salt
freshly ground black pepper
4 shakes cayenne pepper
45 ml [3 tablespoons] thick
 cream (optional)

For the garnish:
3 hard-boiled eggs, quartered
 lengthways
parsley sprigs

1 Put the rice and salt into 575 ml [1 pt] cold water in a saucepan, bring to the boil, stir, cover tightly and cook gently for 15-20 minutes, until all the water has been absorbed and the rice is dry and fluffy.

2 Meanwhile peel and finely chop the onion.

3 Melt 50 g [2 oz] butter in a large saucepan and fry the onion very gently until soft but uncoloured.

4 Free the fish of all skin and bone and flake it with a fork.

5 Remove the white from one of the hard-boiled eggs and chop it roughly. Reserve the yolk.

6 Add the cooked rice, salmon, chopped egg white, chives and remaining butter to the onion, with seasonings of salt, pepper and cayenne pepper.

7 Toss together lightly with a fork and heat gently until hot through.

8 Check the seasoning and stir in the cream if used.

9 Pile on to a hot serving dish, press the reserved hard-boiled egg yolk through a sieve to garnish the top, and surround the base with alternate quarters of hard-boiled egg and sprigs of parsley.

Canny ways with fish

When you want a tasty meal in a hurry, when you feel too tired to go shopping, or when unexpected guests arrive and you need to extend what was planned to be a family meal . . . that's the time to turn to your store cupboard. Take a tip from the ideas given here and use your cunning to turn a can of fish into a splendid and appetizing dish!

Most prudent cooks keep well-stocked store cupboards, so they never run out of everyday basic foods such as flour, sugar, tea, coffee, jam, herbs and spices. But cooks who are both well organized and shrewd see to it that their store cupboard shelves also include a good selection of canned fish. Convenience foods are clearly a boon when it comes to coping with an emergency, and few canned goods keep as well or prove quite so useful as canned fish.

Canned fish is nutritious food and it is marvellously easy to use—no lengthy preparation or cooking is needed—all of which means it is the perfect standby for making interesting hors d'oeuvres, savouries or main course salads at very short notice.

It is worth spending time and imagination on canned fish and you will find that it is very versatile: its flavour and texture go well with so many other foods, so it is a pity to serve it always plain and simple, just as it comes out of a can. You can use it to create delicious sauces, to form the basis of many tasty composite dishes and to add sparkle to lots more: some substantial enough to please a hungry family and some delicate and decorative party dishes to delight your guests.

TYPES, STORAGE AND USES

Canning is a good method of preserving fish and, apart from being neatly packaged, it also has a long shelf-life. Providing your store cupboard is cool and dry, fish canned in tomato sauce will keep well for at least a year, canned in natural juices it will remain in good condition for two years, and fish canned in oil will retain excellent eating qualities for up to five years. Although not essential, it helps the maturing process of fish canned in oil if the cans are turned over at six-monthly intervals.

Anchovy fillets. The best anchovies come from the Bay of Biscay. They are salted for six months before being skinned, filleted and packaged in olive oil in long narrow cans. For certain dishes, and for people who don't like salty foods, it is a good idea to soak anchovies in milk or (cheaper and quicker) to rinse them under cold running water before use.

Almost more than any other fish, anchovy lends zest and dramatic interest to a host of different dishes. Cut them in half lengthways and arrange in lattice patterns, roll them neatly, snip them into little pieces or pound them in a mortar with a pestle for pasties and sauces.

Brisling. These are often described as sardines, but in fact they are sprats which are members of the herring family (brisling is the Norwegian word for sprats). They are much smaller than sardines—averaging 16-24 fish to a 100 g [$\frac{1}{4}$ lb] can. They are lightly smoked before canning and make a good alternative to sardines in hors d'oeuvres and savoury dishes.

Crab. This is a very tasty shellfish and quite a bit cheaper than lobster. The white meat is canned in its natural juices and various graded qualities are sold. Dressed crab contains other ingredients and is suitable for salads. Use pure crab-meat for mousses and pâtés and hot savouries and hors d'oeuvres.

Herrings. These are canned in various forms including small whole fish, fillets and also soft herring roes. Fillets in oil or natural juices are useful for salads, open sandwiches and cooked dishes. Fillets in various savoury sauces can be simply heated through and served on hot toast, or added to rice and vegetable dishes for pilafs.

Soft roes are taken from mature male fish found mostly off the Norwegian coast during the early months of the year. Dipped in seasoned flour, carefully fried then served on buttery toast, they make a traditional British savoury.

Kippers. Like herrings, these are available in cans whole or, more often, filleted. They are useful for salads, hors d'oeuvres and snacks.

Lobster. Usually considered the king of shellfish, canned lobster is not quite as tasty as freshly boiled lobster. The flavour and texture of fresh lobster is probably shown off to best advantage when served plain and unadorned as lobster salad. It makes sense, however, to use the canned variety to bind in sauces (where flavour will be affected by the addition of other ingredients) for filling vol-au-vents to make soufflés, mousses and seafood risotto.

Mackerel. Cuts of mackerel canned in natural juices have proved a popular and inexpensive product. They are excellent for pâtés and salads. Fillets in white wine can be served as an hors d'oeuvre.

Pilchards. Larger and meatier than sardines, these are usually canned in tomato sauce. Good value for money, they are very useful for main meal salads, substantial snacks and cooked dishes.

Prawns and shrimps. Usually canned in natural juices, these small shellfish are great favourites. They look decorative too, which makes them a good choice for garnishing soups and canapés. Use them to make your own prawn paste and to add a touch of class and colour to sauces for poached or baked fish.

Pressed cod's roe. Hard roes are taken from large North Sea cod and cooked in the can. Serve cold in slices, or slice and fry.

Salmon. Various species are caught for canning with the result that there is a variety of grades and prices to choose from. So-called red salmon has the most flavour and is the most expensive and a pink salmon is the cheapest. Use the best salmon for salads, mousses and other cold dishes, and the cheaper grades for cooked dishes.

Sardines. These are small pilchards mostly caught off the north-west coast of Africa and Portugal. After preparation, they are lightly cooked in olive oil, and then canned in the same oil. Cans of Brittany sardines sometimes include a few slices of onion and carrot used in the cooking process to add extra flavour. Sardines are sometimes canned in tomato sauce and these make tasty hot snacks on toast.

The fish vary in size, averaging 4-8 fish to a 100 g [$\frac{1}{4}$ lb] can. The best and most expensive sardines are matured in the can for at least a year before they are to be sold.

Sild. These are similar to brisling but are even smaller. Like brisling, they can be used instead of sardines in many dishes.

Smoked oysters and mussels. Canned in oil, these rich-tasting and exotic seafoods are delicious in bacon rolls, to serve on sticks for snacks or to add to a fish pie to give it a lift.

Tuna. This is the generic name for several related species of fast swimming fish caught in many parts of the world. The best varieties have a soft, tender texture when canned. The very finest and most expensive comes from the underpart of the fish known as 'ventresca'. Tuna has many uses in the kitchen, for sauces, salads and pâtés as well as hot dishes.

QUICK IDEAS

● For sardine bites, drain the oil from sardines, spread the fish with a little French mustard, dip in an egg and breadcrumb mixture and deep fry. Serve with wedges of lemon for an appetizer or to accompany cocktails.

● Chop anchovy fillets finely and add them to lemon and parsley stuffing for extra piquancy. This is excellent with fish, veal and rabbit.

● For eggs with shrimps, a simple but luxurious first course, put a few canned and drained shrimps in cocotte dishes before adding eggs, seasoning and cream. Bake in a bain-marie.

● Summer seafood salad makes an attractive main course for a summer lunch party. Stir some vinaigrette dressing into 225 g [½ lb] cold, boiled rice. Mix in a good handful of finely chopped herbs such as parsley, chives and dillweed, 50 g [2 oz] each of cooked peas and diced cucumber. Arrange in a ring around the edge of the dish. Mix together 50 g [2 oz] sliced raw button mushrooms, 100 g [¼ lb] peeled, seeded and quartered tomatoes and 200 g [7 oz] of flaked crabmeat. Coat lightly with mayonnaise and pile into the centre of the dish. Arrange 75 g [3 oz] canned prawns decoratively on top. Serve with watercress salad.

● For a warming and inexpensive supper make pilchard potatoes. Bake very large potatoes until tender. Cut off the tops and carefully scoop out most of the flesh. Mash this together with pilchards in tomato sauce and season well with salt and pepper. Pile the mixture back into the potato skins and top with a little grated cheese. Return to the oven to heat through and allow the cheese to melt.

● Drained tuna in mayonnaise with a pinch of black pepper and the juice of half a lemon makes an unusual filling for avocado pears.

● For seafarer's rarebit—a tasty snack for anyone who is really hungry—wrap brisling in thin rashers of streaky bacon, grill, then serve on top of cheese on toast.

● Serve grilled bacon and brisling on cocktail sticks for an unusual nibble to accompany aperitifs.

● Tuna and anchovies combine well with French beans, lettuce, cold cooked potatoes, tomatoes, olives and capers for a delicious salade niçoise.

● Almost any canned fish can be used for stuffed eggs. Mash the fish, mix with sieved hard-boiled egg yolks and either a little cream, sour cream, butter or mayonnaise, until of piping consistency. Add complementary seasonings and use to fill halved hard-boiled egg whites.

● Omit egg yolks from the above mixture and use it as a party dip for crisps, potato sticks or crudités.

● For sardine fish cakes, mash drained canned sardines with a squeeze of lemon juice and mix with well-seasoned mashed potato. Form into small rounds, dust with flour and fry. These are very popular with children. Use sild or brisling instead of sardines, if you wish.

● Salmon kedgeree makes a substantial brunch. Stir boiled rice into a pan of melted butter over low heat. Add some thick cream, plenty of freshly chopped chives, parsley, and salt and black pepper. Stir to mix well and allow to become very hot. Gently incorporate canned, drained and flaked pink salmon and chopped hard-boiled eggs just before serving.

● Pound anchovy fillets to a paste, mix with softened butter and spread on rounds of hot toast. On top place grilled or fried tournedos or noisettes of lamb. A cheaper alternative is to spread the mixture on fingers of toast to serve with boiled eggs.

● For tuna bake, mix together a can of flaked tuna fish, a can of sweetcorn kernels and a can of pimentos, all well drained. Stir the mixture into a cheese sauce flavoured with a little nutmeg. Top with breadcrumbs and grated cheese and bake until very hot and golden and bubbling on top.

ANCHOVY AND POTATO PIE

Here is a delicious and unusual dish in which commonplace ingredients are given a lift by the piquancy of anchovies and the richness of cream. Serve it as a supper dish for three or as a vegetable accompaniment to a main course dish of grilled fish, in which case it is sufficient for six.

SERVES 3-6
50 g [2 oz] canned anchovy fillets
3 leeks
40 g [1½ oz] butter
4 tomatoes
550 g [1¼ lb] potatoes
freshly ground black pepper
250 ml [½ pt] chicken stock
150 ml [¼ pt] thin cream

1 Heat the oven to 200°C [400°F] gas mark 6.

2 Drain the anchovies and rinse well under cold running water to get rid of excess salt. Pat dry and set aside.

3 Wash, trim and finely slice the leeks, using tender green parts as well as the white stems.

4 Melt 25 g [1 oz] butter in a small pan, add the leeks, cover and sweat over low heat for about 10 minutes, shaking the pan or stirring from time to time to prevent sticking.

5 Meanwhile, skin and slice the tomatoes, and peel and slice the potatoes very thinly.

6 Use the remaining butter to grease the base and sides of a large shallow dish.

7 Cover the bottom of the dish with a layer of potato slices, using about one-third of the potatoes. Spread half the leeks on top, season with pepper (but not salt because the anchovies contain plenty). Add half the sliced tomatoes and arrange half the anchovies on top.

8 Repeat with another layer of potatoes, the remaining leeks, tomatoes and anchovies, and top with a layer of potatoes.

9 Bring the stock to boiling point and pour it over the dish. Press the mixture down well (a potato masher is the best implement to use for this).

10 Bake in the centre of the oven for 1 hour, occasionally pressing the mixture down into the liquid. By the end of cooking time, the potatoes should be quite tender and have absorbed most of the liquid.

11 Turn off heat and remove dish from oven. Pour the cream over the dish and shake the dish gently so that the cream can seep down to the lower layers.

12 Return the dish to the oven for about 10 minutes to allow the cream to become hot and to be absorbed by the vegetables.

TONNO E FAGIOLI

This classic Italian salad can be served as a hearty appetizer for six to eight (it is filling so the main course which follows should be light). It will make a main course salad for four in which case baked potatoes filled with anchovy butter make a tasty accompaniment. If you want to stretch the dish further to feed an extra person, add any of the following: black olives, sliced hard-boiled eggs, left-over cooked rice or peas but the contrast between fish, nutty beans and cool cucumber is best left alone.

SERVES 4
200 g [7 oz] canned tuna
425 g [15 oz] canned red kidney beans
1 small onion
1 small cucumber
2.5 ml [½ teaspoon] dried dillweed
60 ml [4 tablespoons] freshly chopped parsley
75 ml [3 fl oz] vinaigrette dressing

In Portuguese pâté the richness of sardines is balanced with mustard and lemon juice.

1 Rinse the kidney beans under cold running water. Drain thoroughly and turn the kidney beans into a salad bowl.

2 Peel and chop the onion finely. Cut the cucumber into large dice but do not peel it.

3 Add the vegetables and herbs to the salad bowl. Pour on vinaigrette dressing well flavoured with salt and pepper. Toss the mixture until well coated.

4 Drain the tuna fish, flake it and add it to the salad bowl.

5 Mix lightly and serve.

PORTUGUESE PATE

This sardine pâté is marvellously quick and easy to make. The sharp flavours of mustard, lemon and onion act as an excellent foil for the richness of sardines and combine to produce a tasty hors d'oeuvre at reasonable cost. Serve the pâté garnished with slices of lemon and accompany it with fingers of hot buttered toast sprinkled with chopped parsley.

SERVES 6-8
225 g [½ lb] canned sardines in oil
20 ml [4 teaspoons] French mustard
20 ml [4 teaspoons] lemon juice
45 ml [3 tablespoons] curd cheese
salt and pepper
1 shallot or pickling onion

1 Drain the oil from the sardines, turn the fish into a mixing bowl and mash to a pulp with a fork.

2 Stir the mustard and lemon juice into the curd cheese, then add this mixture to the bowl.

3 Season with salt and pepper and mash again until a smooth paste is achieved and flavours are well blonded.

4 Peel and grate or very finely chop the shallot or pickling onion. Stir it into the pâté.

5 Scrape the bowl clean with a rubber or plastic spatula and pack the pâté into a small dish.

6 Garnish and serve immediately or cover (ungarnished) and refrigerate until required. The pâté will keep for 24 hours.

Variation

● Substitute 4-6 finely chopped spring onions for the shallot or pickling onion and use mayonnaise instead of curd cheese.

KIPPER COCKTAIL

Cheaper and more original than shrimp or prawn cocktail, this makes an elegant appetizer. Serve it in small wine or sherry glasses. Stand each glass on a small plate with a teaspoon for eating the cocktail. Serve with brown bread and butter rolls. Make these using thin slices of buttered, fresh bread with crusts removed and roll up tightly like miniature swiss rolls.

SERVES 6
**200 g [7 oz] canned kipper
   fillets
150 ml [¼ pt] sour cream
half a lemon
15 ml [1 tablespoon] tomato
   ketchup
10 ml [2 teaspoons] French
   mustard
45 ml [3 tablespoons]
   mayonnaise
salt and pepper
2 large dessert apples
3 celery sticks
50 g [2 oz] cashew nuts
parsley sprigs or celery tops**

1 Drain the kippers and cut the flesh into fairly small pieces.

2 Turn the sour cream into a mixing bowl and beat with a fork until smooth and creamy.

3 Grate the lemon zest and add it to the sour cream together with the ketchup, mustard and mayonnaise.

4 Stir to mix well. Season to taste with salt and pepper and mix again.

5 Peel and core the apples and cut into small chunks. Put into a bowl

with the kippers and sprinkle with a little lemon juice to prevent discolouration.

6 Clean and slice the celery and add it to the kipper and apple mixture together with half the nuts.

7 Pour the sauce over and toss lightly to coat all the ingredients.

8 Divide the mixture between six glasses. Cover and chill for 1 hour—but no longer than 3 hours or the nuts will be softened by the sauce.

9 Garnish with remaining nuts and parsley or celery just before serving.

SCALLOPED CRAB

Here is a first course dish which is really in the luxury class. Use canned lobster or prawns instead of crab if you wish. Serve in scallop shells, ramekins or individual soufflé dishes.

SERVES 6
**400 g [14 oz] canned crabmeat
45 ml [3 tablespoons] sherry or
   brandy
60 ml [4 tablespoons] butter
30 ml [2 tablespoons] plain
   flour
250 ml [½ pt] thick cream
30 ml [2 tablespoons] grated
   Parmesan cheese
salt and pepper
freshly grated nutmeg
50 ml [2 oz] toasted
   breadcrumbs**

1 Drain the crabmeat, (reserve juices) put it into a bowl, sprinkle with sherry or brandy.

2 Melt half the butter in a small heavy-based saucepan and make a thick white sauce with the flour and cream adding the cream very gradually.

3 Gently stir in the crabmeat and its can juices. Cover and simmer very gently for 5-10 minutes so that the crabmeat heats through.

4 Meanwhile heat the grill to very hot and grease the scallop shells or dishes with a little butter.

5 Remove the saucepan from the heat. Stir in the grated Parmesan

cheese and season to taste with salt, pepper and nutmeg.

6 Divide the contents of the saucepan between the shells or dishes. Scatter the breadcrumbs over the shellfish mixture and top with the remaining butter cut into flecks.

7 Cook under the grill for 1-2 minutes until browned and very hot, then serve immediately.

SURPRISE MACARONI

Macaroni cheese is cheap, easy to make and very filling—a favourite mid-week dish in many households. This variation on the traditional recipe gives you extra colour, flavour and nutritive value. Make the cheese sauce by making a basic white sauce and stirring in grated Cheddar cheese.

SERVES 4
**200 g [7 oz] canned pilchards
   in tomato sauce
175 g [6 oz] macaroni
1.5 ml [¼ teaspoon] salt
15 ml [1 tablespoon] oil
550 ml [1 pt] cheese sauce
225 g [½ lb] tomatoes
50 g [2 oz] Cheddar cheese**

1 Turn the pilchards and their tomato sauce into a flameproof dish, cover the dish with foil and place in a low oven to heat through while you cook the macaroni and make the cheese sauce.

2 Bring a large pan of water to boiling point. Stir in the macaroni plus the salt for flavour and add the oil to prevent the pasta from sticking together. Cook at a fast boil until tender.

3 Slice the tomatoes, grate the cheese and heat the grill.

4 Turn the cooked macaroni into a colander to strain off all liquid, then stir the drained macaroni into the cheese sauce.

5 Remove the pilchard dish from the oven, uncover and spoon the macaroni cheese on top.

6 Arrange the sliced tomatoes in a layer over the macaroni and top the dish by sprinkling on the cheese.

7 Brown the dish under a hot grill.

Fishing for compliments

Nothing beats an appetizer of smoked fish or roes when you want to give your meal a distinctive air of opulence. Smoked salmon and osetr caviare are clearly in the luxury price bracket and, therefore, reserved for the occasional splash. But humbler goodies such as smoked mackerel, kippers, mock caviare and cod's roe are affordable more often and can easily be made into elegant dishes. Learn how to choose and serve all sorts of smoked fish and roes for the maximum delight of diners and with minimum fuss for the cook.

LUXURIOUS ROES

Hard roe is the egg sack of the female fish and is made up of numerous tiny eggs. Soft roe comes from the male fish and is never smoked. Roe is always impressive as an appetizer, whether it is the expensive caviare or the more modest smoked cod's roe which can be used in a number of ways.

Caviare

This is the salted hard roe of a sturgeon. Large sturgeons are now found only in the Caspian Sea so caviare is almost exclusively a Russian and Iranian product and, consequently, it is extremely expensive.

To be enjoyed at its best you need to eat caviare as fresh as possible. Needless to say, most people have to be content with the slightly muted flavour of pasteurized caviare from pots and cans from specialist food stores.

The three kinds of true caviare are named after the species of sturgeon that supplies the roe—beluga, osetr and sevruga.

Beluga comes from the largest fish (between 16 and 20 years old) and is the most expensive. Colour varies from pale grey to pitch black and the grains are large.

Osetr comes from slightly smaller fish and is the rarest. It has a stronger flavour than beluga. The colour can vary from golden brown through to grey, green and black.

Sevruga comes from smaller (7-10 year old) fish and the grains are therefore smaller too. It has a superb flavour, is the most readily available and is also the cheapest.

Pressed caviare. This is made from left-over roes of various species of sturgeon and pressed into tins. The flavour is very good although more

heavily salted than fresh caviare. It is much less expensive than fresh caviare and is widely used by caterers for fillings and garnishes.

Mock caviare
Mock caviare comes from the roe of fish, such as cod and salmon, as opposed to sturgeon.

Red caviare comes from salmon and it is greatly appreciated for its beautiful golden-red colour. Its taste is unlike true caviare but it has a good individual flavour of its own – somewhere between smoked cod's roe and a fine kipper. It makes stylish cocktail snacks or a tasty filling with sour cream for blini (pancakes).

Lumpfish caviare is a black-or red-dyed mock caviare produced from the roe of the lumpfish. Although it is nothing like caviare in flavour, it makes a dramatic garnish to smoked salmon canapés and open sandwiches and can be used to decorate cold savoury mousses. It is widely available in small pots at relatively modest cost.

Other roes
Botargo is the salted and dried roe of the grey mullet which is native to Mediterranean countries. It is recognizable by its black skin and orange-brown centre. The roe can be served cut into thin slices with bread, olive oil or butter, and a slice of lemon or a fresh fig.

Smoked cod's roe is the firm roe of a large cod which is lightly brined and smoked. It is sold by weight and available from fishmongers. The skin colour of cod's roe can vary a great deal according to the smoker, but the roe should feel soft when pressed otherwise it may be hard and wasteful. If too salty, cod's roe can be soaked in water. Smoked cod's roe is also sold skinned and ready to use in jars. This saves on preparation time and makes a useful store cupboard item for emergencies, but it is an extravagant way to buy smoked cod's roe, which is really very easy to prepare yourself.

Serving caviare
Once bought, the important thing is always to keep fresh, pasteurized or mock caviare chilled but not frozen. Keep it just below the frozen food compartment in a refrigerator and eat it within a day or two.

To appreciate fully the fine flavour of real caviare it should be served

Sevruga

Smoked cod's roe

Red lumpfish caviare

Beluga

Black lumpfish caviare

Red caviare

Pressed caviare

absolutely alone and unadorned, with nothing except a dry biscuit or thin toast. Send it to the table in its container surrounded with ice-cubes. For an average portion allow 25-40 g [1-1½ oz]. Pressed caviare can be served on small dry biscuits as cocktail snacks.

SMOKED FISH
Fish loses its freshness very quickly and can be dangerous if eaten when stale. The eating period can be extended if fish is treated immediately after it is caught. Preservation methods include salting, pickling, smoking, drying, freezing and canning.

The oldest method is brining (immersing fish in heavily salted water) and this process is still used today to tenderize, flavour and preserve fish. Oily fish need more than brine to preserve them if they are to be kept for any length of time so they are smoked afterwards, which also flavours the fish. In fact it gives fish such a delicious piquant taste that even non-oily fish which do not need the additional preservatives are often smoked simply for the flavour.

Smoked fish provide one of the best possible first courses to any meal, and even modest varieties such as mackerel and buckling have an air of opulence.

Although the principles of different types of curing and smoking are basically similar, the same species of fish tastes different when bought from different smokers. So shop around to find the cure most to your liking.

There are two main methods of smoking fish—at a high or relatively low temperature.

Hot-smoked fish. After brining, the fish is smoked in a kiln with the temperature raised to a degree high enough to cook the fish right through. Fish smoked in this way can be served without further cooking. They include buckling, trout and eel, all of which are usually available from delicatessens and fishmongers.

Cold-smoked fish. After brining, the fish is smoked at a relatively low temperature. Most fish prepared in this way need to be lightly cooked before eating. They include haddock, bloater, kipper, whiting and fillets of cod.

Inevitably there are exceptions to these rules. Smoked salmon, which is cold smoked, is nearly always served without further cooking. And some hot-smoked fish, such as Arbroath smokies, although technically completely cooked, are at their most palatable if just heated through before serving.

Choosing and storing smoked fish
The flavour of smoked fish is best when freshly cured, so when buying always look for signs of freshness. These are (as shown in the picture) firm flesh, glossy skin and a wholesome fresh smoked smell. Avoid tired-looking fish that has shrivelled and lost its bloom.

Before the days of refrigeration, heavy salting and prolonged smoking were necessary to preserve fish. Nowadays brining and smoking are light as they are intended mainly as a means of giving fish a delicious flavour. The preservative effect is slight. Therefore smoked fish should be refrigerated and kept for not much longer than the fresh equivalent.

SMOKED FISH

Type and description	Serving ideas
Smoked eel: a rich and satisfying fish with a firm buttery texture. Look for a meaty eel and avoid skinny or dried up specimens. Eel can sometimes be bought filleted in long strips.	Allow about 40 g [1½ oz] per portion. To serve, peel off the skin, ease the two fillets off the bone and arrange side by side on a plate with a wedge of lemon and a sprig of parsley. Serve brown bread and butter separately.
(1) **Smoked salmon:** there are various qualities which account for the varying prices. Top quality smoked Scotch and Irish salmon is relatively pale in colour with dense glossy flesh. Canadian is much brighter in colour and less oily. It is the cheapest and the least good quality. Salmon can be bought as a whole side, in vacuum packs, canned or by weight.	All smoked salmon is best sliced freshly and very thinly, straight from a whole side. Allow 100 g [¼ lb] for 3-4 portions as hors d'oeuvres. Serve with a piece of lemon and have a pepper mill on the table. Paper-thin slices of buttered brown bread, decrusted and rolled, are the best accompaniment. End pieces of smoked salmon can sometimes be bought more cheaply and these do excellently for making canapés, pâtés, stuffed eggs and quiches.
Smoked sturgeon: a seasonal fish, not always available, provides a rare treat. The roe from some of this family is salted and known as caviare.	Slice and serve as for smoked salmon.
(2) **Smoked trout:** a delicately flavoured fish prepared by hot smoking. It must be fresh and succulent to be enjoyed at its best.	Allow 175-200 g [6-7 oz] trout per person. Remove the skin just before serving (not before or the flesh may dry up) but leave the head and tail on. Serve with lemon quarters and buttered brown bread. A light horseradish cream enhances the flavour. Makes an excellent pâté.
(3) **Smoked mackerel:** a new product and one of the great success stories of the modern fishing industry. Hot-smoked mackerel is ready to serve and has a delicious flavour. A cold-smoked mackerel is also available but needs light cooking.	One smallish fillet weighing 75-100 g [3-4 oz] makes an ample portion. Head, tail, skin and bone the fish and serve with lemon and brown bread and butter. It makes excellent salads and pâtés.
(4) **Smoked haddock:** a cure originally developed in the village of Findon in Scotland, where whole haddock were first split open and smoked.	Grilled or lightly boiled, it can be served with cucumber or mayonnaise.
Arbroath smokies: small haddock, beheaded and gutted but left whole and hot smoked.	Can be eaten as it is or brushed with butter and heated through under the grill before serving.
Buckling: the aristocrat of the smoked herring tribe. The fish is beheaded and gutted, and then hot smoked until the skin has a beautiful golden sheen.	Skin the buckling and serve it whole or, if large, filleted. The skin will peel off easily if you cover the fish with boiling water for a minute and then drain it. Buckling makes an excellent pâté and is good in salads.
Bloater: a Yarmouth herring speciality which is rather difficult to find.	It must be lightly grilled or baked within 24 hours of buying.
(5) **Kipper:** a fine fat herring which is split, lightly brined and then cold smoked over wood chips. Available whole, boned, filleted and as 'boil-in-the-bag' and canned products. It is customary for producers to dye kippers, but undyed kippers can still be found in speciality shops.	Marinated in lemon or vinegar, kipper fillets are superb served raw, but to do this safely the kippers must be very fresh. Kippers are also excellent grilled or lightly boiled. Keep kippers refrigerated and use within 5 days.
(6) **Smoked sprats:** a good, relatively cheap and very tasty mouthful from the herring family. Fiddly to eat so you will win laurels if you manage to fillet and skin them first.	Serve with plenty of lemon and brown bread and butter. They can be heated under the grill for a few minutes if preferred hot.

Step-by-step to filleting smoked mackerel

1 Cut off the tail and, if the head is present, remove that too.

2 Cut through the skin along the length of the back.

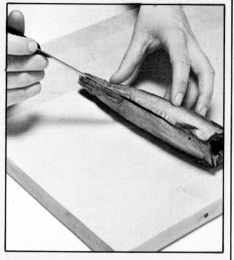

3 Cut through the skin from the end of belly cavity to the tail.

4 Lift skin with the tip of a knife and peel it back.

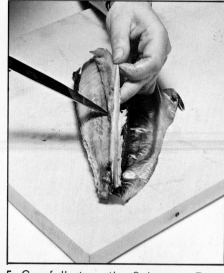

5 Carefully turn the fish over. Peel skin off the other side.

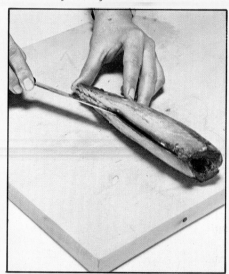

6 Cut through the flesh from the belly cavity to the tail end.

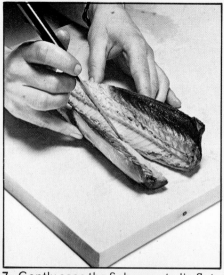

7 Gently ease the fish open to lie flat, exposing the backbone.

8 Lift out the backbone starting at the head end.

9 Scrape away the dark skin of the belly cavity and remaining bones.

SERVING SMOKED FISH

The classic way to serve smoked fish is very simple: with wedges of juicy lemon to season it and brown bread and butter as an accompaniment. This is not only a treat for diners but a sheer delight for the cook since so little work is involved. Diners can either skin and fillet the fish themselves or this can be done in advance, which is very easy as shown in the step-by-step pictures.

For the richer, oilier smoked fish, such as mackerel and buckling, it is a good idea to serve an accompanying sharply flavoured sauce—either as a substitute for or in addition to wedges of lemon. Two delicious cold sauces are given in the recipe section.

Some smoked fish can be marinated to make delicious salads and various types make excellent bases for pâtés, creams and mousses. These are all popular first courses and are equally useful for buffet parties and to accompany drinks, topping cocktail canapés, filling miniature pastry cases, stuffing celery 'boats' and so on.

The richest pâtés are simply made from skinned and filleted fish pounded with unsalted butter and seasoning. Lighter textured, less rich mixtures can be made by replacing some of the butter with cream, cream cheese, cottage cheese, hard-boiled egg, or even a small proportion of fresh breadcrumbs (which also makes the pâté go a little further).

HORSERADISH CREAM

This piquant cream requires no cooking and makes a delicious accompaniment to smoked fish. If you are unable to get fresh horseradish, use 30 ml [2 tablespoons] bottled horseradish sauce instead.

SERVES 6-8
fresh horseradish
150 ml [5 fl oz] thick cream
30 ml [2 tablespoons] milk
5 ml [1 teaspoon] lemon juice
salt
2.5 ml [½ teaspoon] sugar

1 Peel and finely grate the horseradish to yield 15 ml [1 tablespoon].

2 Pour the milk and the cream into a small basin and whisk until thick but not stiff.

3 Stir in the lemon juice, horseradish, salt and sugar.

4 Serve lightly chilled.

Variation
● For mustard cream, substitute 15 ml [1 tablespoon] English mustard for the horseradish.

SMOKED MACKEREL MONACO

The richness of smoked mackerel is beautifully contrasted with a sharp crunchy salad of raw celery, apple and sour cream. This is a rich dish so there is no need for large portions.

SERVES 4
450 g [1 lb] smoked mackerel
2 crisp dessert apples
22.5 ml [1½ tablespoons] lemon juice
3 celery sticks
150 ml [¼ pt] sour cream
freshly ground black pepper

For the garnish:
half a small sweet red pepper or canned pimento
30 ml [2 tablespoons] freshly chopped parsley

1 Cut off the head and tail of the mackerel. Carefully cut through the skin along the length of the belly and the back and remove the skin.

2 Open the mackerel and lift out the backbone and as many of the small bones as possible.

3 Using two forks, break up the mackerel flesh into small rough chunks about the size of sugar lumps.

4 Wash the apples, quarter them and remove the cores but do not peel.

5 Chop the apples into fairly small dice. Put into a basin with the lemon juice and stir thoroughly. The lemon prevents the apples from discolouring.

6 Clean the celery sticks and chop into pieces the same size as the apples.

7 Add the celery to the apples, pour over sour cream and add a good grinding of pepper. Mix together.

8 Divide the sour cream mixture into 4 portions and spoon on to four small plates.

9 Divide the mackerel into 4 portions and arrange the chunks around the sour cream mixture.

10 Cut the red pepper into thin strips, discarding pith and seeds, or drain and thinly slice the canned pimento.

11 Criss-cross the strips of red pepper or pimento on the mackerel and sprinkle the chopped parsley over the sour cream mixture.

SMOKED FISH APPETIZER

This hors d'oeuvre is a selection of smoked fish divided into portions and arranged on an individual plate for each person. Prepare the fish as neatly as possible, arrange it on the plates in a uniform pattern and the result will be an enticing start to a meal.

SERVES 6
50 g [2 oz] smoked salmon, thinly sliced
1 small smoked trout or buckling
1 small smoked mackerel
3-4 marinated kipper fillets (see recipe on following page)

For the garnish:
1 lemon
1 seedless orange
12 small gherkins
watercress sprigs

1 Divide the salmon into 6 and form the slices into rolls.

2 Skin and fillet the trout (or buckling) and cut each fillet into 3 portions.

3 Skin and fillet the mackerel and cut into very small, rough-shaped pieces.

4 Drain the kipper fillets from the marinade and cut each across into strips about 1 cm [⅓"] wide. Use scissors to do this as it is easier than using a knife.

5 Arrange a portion of each type of fish on each plate.

Tasty first courses: smoked trout pâté with lemon twists, buckling-stuffed lemons and marinated kipper fillets.

6 Wipe the fruit clean and cut each into 6 segments.

7 Cut the gherkins into fans and wash and drain the watercress.

8 Garnish each plate with gherkins, watercress, lemon and orange.

BUCKLING-STUFFED LEMONS

The inclusion of butter makes this pâté very rich. It is best accompanied by slender fingers of hot, freshly made toast. The mixture is too thick and dry to blend in a liquidizer so you will need a mortar and pestle to make it.

SERVES 4
1 large buckling, about 200 g [7 oz]
4 lemons
100 g [¼ lb] unsalted butter at room temperature
half a garlic clove [optional]
freshly ground black pepper
4 bay leaves

1 Slice the tops off the lemons and set aside. Cut a sliver off the other end of each lemon so they will stand upright.

2 Scoop out the pulp with a tea-

spoon and place in a nylon sieve resting over a small bowl. Press the juice through.

3 Put the buckling in a basin, cover with boiling water and leave to stand for 1 minute.

4 Drain and cut off the tail. Carefully cut through the skin along the length of the belly and the back and peel away skin.

5 Open the fish. Lift out the backbone and as many small bones as possible.

6 Put the fillets into a mortar. Add the butter. Peel and slice the garlic and add.

7 Pound with a pestle until fish and butter have blended and are reduced to a thick smooth paste.

8 Stir in 15 ml [1 tablespoon] of the reserved lemon juice and add a good grinding of black pepper.

9 Check seasoning and add more lemon juice if wished.

10 Spoon the mixture into lemon shells, replace caps and decorate each with a bay leaf. Refrigerate for 30 minutes or until required.

SMOKED TROUT PÂTÉ

This is a delicately flavoured pâté and less rich than most because sour cream and cream cheese are used. The ingredients are blended most easily in a liquidizer. You could use a large pestle and mortar instead but it will take you slightly longer. Serve the pâté in one large dish or six small individual dishes or cocottes. Garnish with lemon twists and serve with crisp dry biscuits.

SERVES 6
2 fresh smoked trout, 175-200 g [6-7 oz] each
150 ml [¼ pt] sour cream
5 ml [1 teaspoon] horseradish sauce
5 ml [1 teaspoon] lemon juice
15 ml [1 tablespoon] freshly chopped parsley
100 g [¼ lb] cream cheese
25 g [1 oz] butter at room temperature
black pepper

1 Cut off the heads and tails from the trout.

2 Carefully cut through the skin along the length of the belly and the back and peel away the skin.

3 Open out the fish and lift the flesh off the backbones, taking care to

remove all the small bones.

4 Put the trout into a liquidizer. Add the sour cream, horseradish sauce, lemon juice and parsley and blend until smooth.

OR pound the smoked trout, a little at a time, in a mortar with a pestle. Stir in the sour cream, horseradish sauce, lemon juice and parsley to make a smooth, creamy paste.

5 Add the cream cheese, butter and pepper and blend again until smooth. Do this either in the liquidizer or by creaming and beating the mixture in a mortar.

6 Check seasoning. Turn the mixture into a large dish or six individual dishes, packing the mixture firmly and smoothing the top with a palette knife. Cover and refrigerate until required.

MARINATED KIPPER FILLETS

You will need four kippers for this dish. It is essential that they are fresh and of top quality. Ask the fishmonger to fillet them as this is a tricky job or buy frozen kipper fillets. The marinade will break down any little bones.

SERVES 4
8 kipper fillets
1 small onion
45 ml [3 tablespoons] lemon juice
60 ml [4 tablespoons] olive oil
6 black peppercorns
2 bay leaves

1 Skin the kipper fillets and remove any obvious bones.

2 Lay the kippers flat in a small dish just large enough to hold them.

3 Peel the onion, slice thinly and lay on top of the kippers.

4 Mix the lemon juice and oil together and pour over the kippers.

5 Tuck the peppercorns and the bay leaves between the fish.

6 Cover and refrigerate overnight.

7 To serve, drain the fillets and serve 2 per portion.

WATERCRESS AND WALNUT SAUCE

Here is another excellent cold sauce to serve with smoked fish. Purists would say that the walnut skins should be rubbed off before making the sauce. This does give a finer flavour but takes hours to do unless the walnuts are very fresh and moist, in which case the skins rub away easily if the shelled nuts are plunged in boiling water for 1 minute.

SERVES 6-8
25 g [1 oz] walnuts, shelled weight
1 bunch watercress
150 ml [¼ pt] sour cream
salt and pepper

1 Put the walnuts, a few at a time, in a mezzaluna or mortar and chop or pound until quite finely ground.

2 Wash the watercress and pull the leaves off the stems. Reserve stalks for soup or stock and plunge the leaves in boiling water for 1 minute.

3 Turn into a sieve to drain and squeeze the watercress dry, then chop finely.

4 Stir the sour cream until smooth and turn into a small mixing bowl.

5 Add the walnuts and watercress and mix well. Season to taste with salt and freshly ground black pepper.

119

HALIBUT MAYONNAISE

Halibut or turbot are both delicious eaten cold with salad. The secret of serving fish cold is to eat it as soon as possible after cooking and cooling, then it will be moist and succulent. Don't therefore, cook it the day before. Halibut steaks from the tail end look attractive and are virtually boneless once the centre bone is removed.

SERVES 4

4 halibut steaks, weighing about 175 g [6 oz] each
salt and white pepper
half a lemon
30 ml [2 tablespoons] of thin cream
200 ml [7 fl oz] home-made mayonnaise
100 g [¼ lb] black grapes
2 seedless oranges
crisp lettuce leaves
watercress sprigs

1 Lightly oil a large piece of kitchen foil or greaseproof paper and lay the fish on it.

2 Season the fish with salt and white pepper. Squeeze the lemon and pour juice over the fish.

3 Wrap the foil round the fish to form a secure parcel and re-frigerate until ready to be cooked.

4 Prepare a steamer and steam fish for 15–20 minutes. Remove parcel and open it to cool the fish.

5 Halve and de-seed the grapes. Peel the oranges and remove pith. Cut the orange in thin slices.

6 Using a fish slice transfer the fish to a wire rack over a dish. Remove the centre bones and skin.

7 Stir the thin cream into the mayonnaise and coat each halibut steak thickly with the mayonnaise.

8 Decorate the coated steaks with the prepared grapes and a sprig of watercress.

9 Line a dish with lettuce leaves. Transfer the fish on to it and garnish with orange slices.

Star recipe
Paella

This traditional one-pot Spanish dish gets its name from the heavy iron frying-pan with two handles in which it is customarily cooked and served. In the absence of a proper paella, use a frying-pan, sauté pan or a wide-bottomed flameproof casserole. However, note that whatever you use it must be large enough to contain 1.4 litres [2½ pt] of stock plus the large quantity of rice in addition to the chicken, shellfish and vegetables. If necessary, divide your ingredients into two pans and cook side by side.

The result is a pretty and colourful party dish, which looks and tastes just as good cold. Saffron is one of the main ingredients of a true paella because of its unique flavour and rich yellow colour. But in this recipe it has been listed as an alternative as it is expensive. Instead turmeric can be used for colouring, although, it must be admitted, the flavour is not quite the same.

SERVES 8
4 chicken joints
15 ml [1 tablespoon] turmeric
   or 4 ml [¾ teaspoon]
   powdered saffron
2 large bay leaves
500 g [1 quart] prawns in
   their shells
225 g [1 pt] shrimps in
   their shells
1 kg [1 quart] mussels in their
   shells
salt
freshly ground black pepper
cooking oil
1 large green pepper
1 large red pepper
2 Spanish onions
4 garlic cloves
350 g [¾ lb] long-grain rice
700 g [1½ lb] tomatoes
125 g [¼ lb] frozen peas

1 Put the chicken joints in a pan. Add the turmeric. If using saffron, dissolve the powder in 15 ml [1 tablespoon] of boiling water but do not add to the pan at this stage.

2 Cover the chicken joints with water and add the bay leaves. Bring the water to the boil, cover and simmer for 25 minutes.

3 When the time is up, take out the chicken joints and discard the bay leaves. Reserve the stock.

4 Shell half the prawns and all the shrimps, reserving the shells.

5 Prepare the mussels (see step-by-step instructions on pages 124–125. If any of the mussel shells are open, given them a sharp tap with the back of a knife. If they do not close, discard them—as this will mean they are dead. Pull away beards, scape off encrustations and scrub shells thoroughly under cold running water. Put the prepared mussels in a saucepan. Cover with water and boil rapidly until they open.

6 Reserving the mussel stock, remove the mussels from the pan and remove top shell. Discard any that have remained closed.

7 Strain the mussel stock through a fine sieve to catch any sand or grit.

8 Skin the chicken and shred the flesh from the bones. Reserve these bones.

9 Measure both the mussel stock and the reserved chicken stock into a large pan and make up to 1.7 L [3 pt] with water. Add the re-

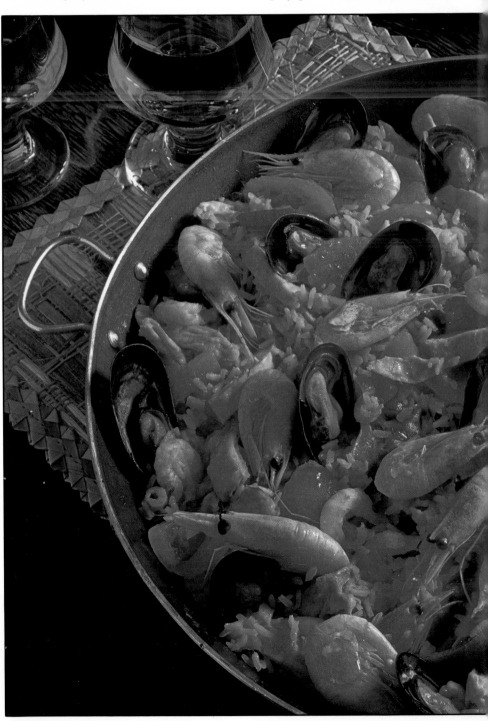

served chicken bones and prawn and shrimp shells to the pan.

10 Boil rapidly until the liquid in the pan has reduced to 1.4 L [2½ pt]. Taste and season with salt and black pepper if necessary.

11 Take the dish in which the paella is to be cooked and cover the bottom with oil. Place over a moderate heat.

12 Rinse, quarter and de-seed the peppers. Cut across into 6 mm [¼"] wide strips. Fry gently in the oil for

2-3 minutes. Take out and reserve.

13 Peel and chop the onion and garlic finely. Fry in the same oil until soft.

14 Pour in the rice and turn over and over in the oil to heat through.

15 Strain the hot reduced stock into the paella pan and add the shredded chicken meat. Stir until the mixture is bubbling.

16 Lower the heat and continue stirring until the rice begins to absorb the stock.

17 Meanwhile scald the tomatoes in a pan of boiling water for 1 minute in order to skin them. Then chop roughly, de-seeding where possible.

18 Stir the chopped tomato into the paella. Add the shelled prawns, shrimps and mussels. If using saffron, add the infused powder at this stage too. Cover the paella pan tightly with foil. Turn to the lowest possible heat and cook gently, without disturbing, for 20 minutes.

19 When the time is up, stir the paella. Add the reserved peppers and the peas and stir again.

20 Strew the remaining prawns (unshelled) over the top. Re-cover tightly with foil and cook for a further 5-10 minutes. By this time the rice should have absorbed all the liquid but still be firm.

21 Serve hot from a paella pan or, if cooking in a substitute pan, transfer to one or two large, warmed serving dishes before taking to the table.

Star recipe

Moules à la marinière

Shellfish add a touch of luxury to any meal; mussels are a great treat and fortunately they do not cost a luxury price.

This dish comes from France's Atlantic coast and is excellent, providing that the mussels are fresh and thoroughly cleaned. Gritty mussels are unpleasant to eat, while sand left in the soup will collect in the liquor, turning it grey. Dead mussels can give you nasty food poisoning, so be sure that they are alive, by the means described here.

Serve moules à la mariniere as a meal-in-a-bowl for two people or a first course for four. For a meal-in-a-bowl buy 1 kg [2¼ lb] of mussels per person if sold by weight, or 1 L [1 qt] if sold by volume.

If a large number of mussels in the fishmonger's tray are open or the shells are broken, do not buy them because these will be dead. (Live mussels usually keep their shells closed when they are out of water.)

When you get home, clean the mussels thoroughly. This is not difficult but it does take time. Keep the cleaned mussels immersed in a bowl of water until required for cooking, changing the water several times.

Eat mussels on the day of purchase whenever possible. If you have to leave them overnight, add some salt to the water. If wished you can add a little flour or oatmeal, too, to feed the mussels so they become plump and white. Cover the bowl with a clean cloth and put in a cool place.

After cooking, check again that your mussels are fresh. Heat should force the shells open so discard any that remain closed.

It is usual to remove half the shell from each mussel before serving. This is to reduce the amount of shell in the soup bowls. Put an empty plate in the centre of the table for the remaining halves of the shells as each person discards them.

Serve in soup bowls with the mussels piled up, and provide spoons for the soup liquid. To eat the mussels, you pick the shell up in your fingers and tip the mussel into your mouth, discarding the empty shell. It is therefore a good idea to provide big napkins to wipe sticky fingers, and finger-bowls would also be useful.

SERVES 2
2 kg [2 quarts] mussels
1 onion
1 shallot (or a second onion)
1 garlic clove
4 parsley stalks
thyme sprig or dried thyme
salt and pepper
40 g [1½ oz] butter
200 ml [7 fl oz] dry white wine
  or dry cider
75 ml [3 fl oz] water
15 ml [1 tablespoon] chopped
  parsley

1 Mussels should be absolutely fresh. Tap any open mussel. Discard it if it does not shut.

5 When ready to cook, drain the mussels. Chop the garlic, onion and shallot very finely.

6 Melt butter in a large saucepan over low heat. Add vegetables, cover and sweat for 10 minutes.

10 Reduce the heat and cook for a further 3 minutes to make sure the mussels are cooked.

11 Strain the liquor through a colander into a second saucepan. Discard the herbs.

2 Using your hands, pull away beards (any hanging seaweed gripped between the two shells).

3 Scrub the mussels under cold running water. Scrape away encrustations with a sharp knife.

4 Keep the mussels in a bowl of cold water until ready to cook. Change the water several times.

7 Tie parsley stalks and thyme with a piece of fine string. Or tie up dried thyme in buttermuslin.

8 Add the herbs, wine or cider and water to the pan. Heat through slowly until almost boiling.

9 Add the mussels, cover and shake gently over fierce heat for 2 minutes to open the shells.

12 Discard any mussels that are still tightly shut. Remove half a shell from each that is open.

13 Add the mussels on their half shells to the liquor in the pan. Reheat gently and season to taste.

14 Ladle soup into a tureen or bowls, heaping up the mussels in the centre. Garnish with parsley.

Star recipe

TARAMASALATA

The name literally means salad of 'tarmara'. This is the salted grey mullet roe but, as this fish is seldom found beyond the Mediterranean, smoked cod's roe makes an excellent substitute.

There are many ways of making taramasalata but the easiest way is to use a liquidizer. If you do not have one, pound the roe with a pestle in a mortar, although it will take longer.

The easiest way to remove the outer skin of the roe is to immerse the roe in boiling water. You lose less roe this way than the alternative method of scraping the soft eggs from the skin with a blunt knife.

Traditionally, taramasalata is served with pita bread but, if this is not available, thin slices of toast or brown bread are perfectly acceptable.

You can turn taramasalata into a dip to serve with crudités by stirring in sour cream to make the basic smoked cod's roe pâté slightly thinner.

SERVES 6
150 g [5 oz] smoked cod's roe
1 thick slice white bread
60 ml [4 tablespoons] water
1 garlic clove
freshly ground black pepper
250 ml [½ pt] olive oil
30 ml [2 tablespoons] lemon juice

For the garnish:
black olives
2 lemons

1 Put the cod's roe in a bowl. Pour on boiling water to cover completely and leave for 1 minute.

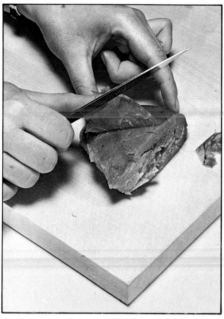

2 Drain the roe. Make a nick in the skin with the point of a sharp knife and peel away skin.

3 Cut crusts from the bread and pour on water. Press with a spoon until bread is soft and pappy.

4 Gently squeeze the bread with your fingers to remove excess liquid and leave a soft white pulp.

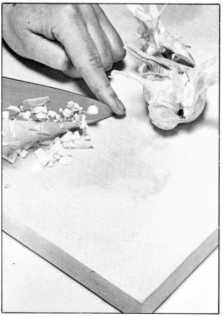

5 Using a sharp knife, peel away garlic skin and chop the flesh into small pieces.

6 Add the garlic, 30 ml [2 tablespoons] oil and some pepper to the bread and blend.